EXTRAORDINARY RELATIONSHIPS

A New Way of Thinking About Human Interactions

D0005673

ROBERTA M. GILBERT, M.D.

CHRONIMED PUBLISHING

Extraordinary Relationships
A New Way of Thinking About Human Interactions © 1992
by Roberta M. Gilbert, MD

Library of Congress Cataloging-in-Publication Data

Gilbert, Roberta M., MD
    Extraordinary relationships: a new way of thinking about human
    interactions / Roberta M. Gilbert, MD
    Includes biographical references and index
    ISBN 1-56561-002-4 $24.95 (hard cover)
    ISBN 1-56561-008-3 $12.95 (paperback)
    1. Interpersonal relations. 2. Social interaction.
    3. Family psychotherapy. I. Title
    HM132.G528   1991
    158' .2--dc20   92-15253
                                                            CIP

Edited by: Patricia Richter
Cover and Interior Design: Dan Norquist
Printed in the United States of America

10 9 8 7 6 5 4

Published by: CHRONIMED Publishing
P.O. Box 47945
Minneapolis, MN 55447-9727

CONTENTS

*To everyone who wants to begin
to think differently about human relationships.*

Foreword—Dr. Michael Kerr

Murray Bowen, M.D., died on October 9, 1990, at his home in Chevy Chase, Maryland. He was 77 years old. A psychiatrist, Bowen had dedicated his life to the "human cause," producing a remarkable new theory of human behavior, *family systems theory*, also known as *Bowen theory*. The new theory has the potential to replace most of Freudian theory and to radically change treatment approaches, not only in psychiatry, but in all of medicine. Potential applications of Bowen theory extend beyond the human family to nonfamily groups, including large organizations and society as a whole. This book by Dr. Roberta Gilbert, who was first a student and later a colleague of Murray Bowen, is an important contribution to understanding his ideas.

Bowen was born in Waverly, Tennessee, on January 31, 1913, the first of five children of Jess Sewell Bowen and Maggie Luff Bowen. The Bowens had a funeral parlor and furniture business in that small Tennessee town, 60 miles west of Nashville. After undergraduate and medical training at the University of Tennessee, internships at two hospitals in New York City, and service in Europe with the army during World War II, Bowen began formal psychiatric training in 1946 at the Menninger Clinic in Topeka, Kansas. After training, he remained there on staff until 1954. From 1954 to 1959, he conducted research on families with a schizophrenic member at the National Institute of Mental Health in Rockville, Maryland. He continued family research and taught at the Georgetown University School of Medicine's Department of Psychiatry in Washington, D.C., from 1959 until his death. Bowen was Clinical Professor of Psychiatry and Director of the Georgetown University Family Center.

Bowen's research and efforts to develop theory were based on the assumption that, in spite of the complexities and vagaries of human existence, *a science of human behavior could be developed.* He believed that a major obstacle to the acceptance of human behavior as a proper subject for scientific inquiry is that, traditionally, humankind has tended to consider itself a unique form of life, one with a special place in God's plan. Such self-glorification precludes our seeing the myriad ways we act just like other forms of life. If we can shift our focus from differences to similarities, we can stay factual about all behavior, human as well as nonhuman. When humans are considered a special case, the floodgates spring open to imagination and subjectivity as a way of explaining what we do.

Although Bowen was convinced that his theory would make a far greater contribution to the human cause than would the new method of psychotherapy that he developed from the theory, the new therapy also radically departs from conventional practice. By approaching therapy differently, many seemingly unchangeable situations acquire new hope.

Understanding the innovations of the new therapy depends on understanding a very basic concept in the theory, namely that the family is an *emotional unit.* The concept of an emotional unit means that any change in the emotional functioning of one family member is predictably and automatically compensated for by changes in the emotional functioning of other family members. This has two important implications: (1) The emotional functioning of every family member plays a part in the occurrence of a medical, psychiatric, or social illness in one family member, and (2) treatment need not be directed at the symptomatic person. Not having to direct treatment at the symptomatic person brings new flexibility to many difficult clinical situations—for example, ones where the symptomatic person either refuses therapy or goes only under great pressure from others.

If any family member can change his or her emotional functioning, provided he or she is present and accounted for within the family, the whole family will improve its functioning in response to that change. In the process, the clinical symptom or relationship problem present in the family will generally lessen. Such a viewpoint provides both solid rationale for *not trying to change others* and guidelines for *being part of the family without being part of the family problem.* Absent a theory that conceptualizes the family as a unit, individuals tend to get frustrated and angry with others and to use those feelings as a justification for calling their families "sick" and cutting off from them. Conversely, some feel guilty about letting their families down and simply withdraw.

Roberta Gilbert is among those who have had considerable firsthand experience with psychoanalytic theory and psychoanalysis and who have made the transition to Bowen's new theories. This is far more difficult than most people might think. When one is schooled in one way of thinking, strongly committed to a professional direction based on that way of thinking, and surrounded by colleagues who reinforce one's position, change does not come easily. Nor does it come easily in the face of society at large, which reflexively blames individuals rather than taking into account all the forces at work in a given problem.

Even Dr. Gilbert thought Bowen was way off base when she first heard him lecture, but eventually she began to "hear." Although well-established as a psychiatrist in Kansas City and busy teaching in two medical schools, she was motivated to learn more about Bowen theory and about herself.

In the early 1980s, Gilbert enrolled in the Special Postgraduate Program in Family Theory and Therapy at the Georgetown Family Center, a program for mental health professionals near Washington, D.C. She began not only learning the new theory but also living it personally and professionally.

She had a gift for it. She knew how much the ideas were contributing to her own life and she watched how much others gained. She felt responsible for doing something about disseminating, not just talking about, the ideas.

In 1987, Dr. Gilbert moved to the Washington, D.C., area to be more closely involved with the Georgetown Family Center. She became a faculty member at the Center and quickly assumed a variety of responsibilities. Her background in psychoanalytic theory made her especially adept at highlighting differences between individual and systems theory, and her skill at articulating these differences is the basis for this book.

One of the book's strengths is the use of detailed clinical descriptions to illustrate abstract theoretical points. Relationship patterns in families, for example, are all variations of a basic theme: anxiety generated by people's difficulty thinking, feeling, and acting for themselves when closely involved with others, especially during periods of heightened stress. The patterns in which anxiety plays out in families are knowable, finite in number, and universal. Dr. Gilbert's descriptions help the patterns jump out at the reader, getting beyond focusing on what is wrong with people—beyond diagnoses, beyond blaming self or others.

Dr. Gilbert also addresses many common questions about the theory and therapy; for example, what does it mean to manage feelings? Some people think that focusing on emotional process, which is an important component of therapy based on Bowen theory, is simply an effort to avoid or bury feelings. How does acting on factual knowledge of an emotional process resolve feelings connected to that process? Gilbert's discussion of such techniques of self-regulation as biofeedback helps to clarify this issue.

In addition to elucidating the basic theory, Gilbert explores its potential to be extended to nonfamily systems. Bowen did some initial work on organizations and the larger society, but there is much more to be done in these areas. Gilbert discusses work and friendship relationships and international relations.

Bowen's theory has been in the medical literature for more than 25 years; he provided a skeleton, a solid skeleton open to change, based on new facts. Dr. Roberta Gilbert's book, focusing as it does on specific aspects of the theory and their applicability to changing relationships, adds detail to the theory and therapy. It elevates psychotherapy from an almost mystical event to a quite understandable process.

For those who can get free enough of conventional notions about human behavior to "hear" something different, the book provides a refreshing alternative to common "self-help" approaches.

Michael E. Kerr, M.D
Director, Georgetown Family Center,
Washington, D.C.

Foreword—Dr. Murray Bowen

Toward Theory

There have been an increasing number of unsolicited communications about the way lives have been changed by Bowen theory. Many have taken the form of "My life has been different since I learned your theory." There were frequent questions, "What was so helpful?" Responses were as personal as the original statement. The wonderment was often discussed in regular theory meetings. Roberta Gilbert, M.D., attended most of the meetings. She did a paper that combined her own personal reasons about the way her professional life changed after learning the theory. It was detailed enough for the Family Center Report, but took the form of a personal testimonial rather than an objective report. As such, it was not publishable. If it were possible to rewrite the paper, eliminate most of the personal pronouns, and put the content into the third person, the theoretical content might qualify for publication. A lesser writer might not have been intrigued by such a rewrite. A new report was submitted within days. It is printed here for the readers.

A good theory is usually an impersonal thing, fashioned from universal knowledge and careful observation. It is usually free of personal pronouns, unless used to convey meaning, or unless there is specific reason to delineate self from others in the field. When the overuse of personal pronouns is avoided, the content is framed in the third person, the writing is more solidly theoretical. People tend to dilute theory with personal feelings. It involves mental health professionals too. The dilution has been called the erosion of theory. The erosion is present even when the theory is clearly expressed. Dr. Gilbert has made a big step in moving from a personal tribute toward an impersonal theory. The basic theory is different from any other in the mental health field. Perhaps the focus on this one small point will help readers separate disguised personal feelings from theoretical facts. It might contribute a little to authors in the future.

From Family Center Report, Spring 1989
Printed with Dr. Bowen's permission

(The paper to which Dr. Bowen referred in this foreword tells a story similar to the preface of this book, although the preface is written in the first person.)

Foreword—Dr. Walter Toman

Historically, Murray Bowen's family therapy must be counted among the earliest practical and teachable forms of psychotherapeutic treatment of families in need and distress.

Viewing the family as a whole in which every individual member affects all others, tracing the members' needs for individuality as well as togetherness, their degrees of differentiation of self and emotional maturity, their relationship patterns and modes of communication, and watching both the system and the process of family life while interacting with the family, have been the hallmarks of Georgetown family therapy. Add exploration of family of origin that the family members are doing for homework, including sibling roles, family constellations, family trees, and communication with all family members. Add, moreover, a family therapist who is attentive and helpful without getting sucked into the family system, and who does not act like a bulldozer shattering the family system or trying to rearrange the rubble. Add free expression for all family members and an obligation to try to listen, and an atmosphere of warm rationality and calm that the family therapist tends to maintain and elicit.

There is no protracted dependence of family members on the therapist, no extensive regression to early levels of differentiation of self and emotional maturity for therapy's sake. On the other hand, there is no exhibition of therapeutic tricks, no show business, no guru power or manipulation of family by decree. But there is all the independence and autonomy that the family and each of its members can muster and stand, and there is all the respect and tact and sensitivity on the part of the therapist that the family needs.

In *Extraordinary Relationships*, Roberta Gilbert has captured Murray Bowen's theoretical and practical assumptions about the family system, its growth, its disturbances and possible therapies splendidly. She writes with competence, great didactic skill, and from a large fund of clinical and psychotherapeutic experience. All her messages are clear and articulate, her practical examples vivid and instructive. This holds also for her concise account of my comprehensive research in family constellation and sibling position and its role in Bowen theory and family therapy.

Summarizing, Dr. Gilbert has written a perfect and unpretentious primer of family relationships. The book is a relief to read, particularly when compared with some of the books on the subject that seem to hide and disguise or confound rather than reveal underlying assumptions, facts, and result, or merely to brag about the fantastic things their authors are doing. Students and even patients of psychotherapy and family therapy will treasure this new book.

Dr. Walter Toman
Professor Emeritus
Erlangen-Nurnberg University
Germany

Preface

When I was first exposed to the ideas of Murray Bowen, I wondered if the world of human behavior really needed another new theory. Most therapists had all they could manage in attempting to master existing theories, to say nothing of staying current with the seemingly endless variations and updated versions.

I had spent many years in practice using the prevailing psychiatric theories and had concluded that my work was useful to most of the people I served. Yet I believed there was some room for improvement. Perhaps I had an imperfect understanding of the theoretical framework out of which I was operating, or a faulty technique, or perhaps the problem was the theoretical framework itself. I wasn't sure just what the problem was.

The careful and painful explorations of my patients' feelings led to no resolution—only to more and more bared feelings that required extended therapy. Psychotherapy, it seemed to me, was without a goal except that of continued introspection. Dependence on the therapist seemed to intensify rather than diminish as people looked for guidance through the "feelings jungle." And I had few resources with which to approach specific relationship problems such as marriage, child rearing, addictions, or physical illness, the very issues most frequently presented to me.

On another level, I looked at the problems of society itself. Crime, divorce, and addiction statistics were climbing. The existence of the institutions of marriage and family seemed threatened. But theories concerning human behavior did not address these concerns. Whenever I tried to apply existing psychiatric ideas to the social arena, I reached dead ends. Indeed, some of the societal problems, it seemed to me, were exacerbated by concepts prevalent in the human-behavior field. Perhaps I could learn a different approach from the small group that was thinking so differently in Georgetown.

Almost as soon as I started studying Bowen theory, I began to apply it in my practice and in my own life. In the beginning I was full of questions and confusion, but I could perceive that I was being exposed to a way of thinking far superior to anything I had previously studied. Gradually, over several years' time, during which I frequently traveled between Washington and Kansas City, the new concepts worked a kind of magic in my life and in my clinical work. As I improved my ability to "think systems," I saw new options for managing myself emotionally. Members of my family sometimes made comments that let me know I was on the right track. Moreover, my patients began to show results in an entirely different league from anything I had seen before.

Still, the process of learning a new way of thinking, one that departs from habituated beliefs, is arduous. Once, during one of my many flights to Washington, I visited a friend, a professor of psychiatry at nearby Johns Hopkins University School of Medicine. He expressed amazement that someone at my stage of life and career would go to so much trouble to learn a new theory. For my part, I found it amazing that the profession of psychiatry was not beating a path to Dr. Bowen's door.

Psychiatry, so far, has yet to embrace Bowen family systems theory. This is understandable. For one thing, psychiatry as a profession is inherently conservative. All life prefers homeostasis to change. Furthermore, the new way of thinking is more complex than the old. Indeed, the shift in thinking from existing psychiatric ideas to Bowen theory is similar to the adjustment asked of a child when told, looking out at a flat horizon, that the earth is round.

Just what is the role of theory in science?

Developing a new theory, a profound and radical act, involves reexamining old assumptions and conclusions. It is, in short, taking the first step into scientific inquiry.

A theory is a building block in the development of scientific knowledge. It begins with observation. Observations that do not fit existing theory lead to the development of new theory. If enough factual data are accumulated to support it, a theory is gradually incorporated into science as fact. The idea of the earth being round was once a theory. But gradually, as astronomical and then navigational data were gathered, the theory of the round earth became recognized as scientific fact. The role of bacteria in disease processes was at first a theory. When the microscope was invented, bacteria were observable, and theory became scientific fact. In biology, the theory of the evolution of species as first proposed by Darwin has gained observational support from so many investigators that, (although some people see conflicts with their basic assumptions) the theory is very close to being recognized universally as scientific fact.

Bowen's ideas are still at the theory stage of scientific development. Based upon his years of observing human behavior as a psychiatrist, Bowen saw that studying the individual alone and even studying his important relationships would never explain all the facts. He postulated no less radical departure from existing theory than that the family system, not the individual, comprises the emotional unit. Therefore, understanding the family system of an individual as completely and broadly as possible would be the most effective way to understand the individual in relationships.

The tremendous success of current books and presentations about relationships and the family is heartening and may indicate that at least a certain segment of the population is ready to explore the world of the emotional relationship system. These books and presentations have made use of Bowen theory along with other theories and systems of thought. They have been immensely useful to very large numbers of people, standing in the important place of opening a door on new possibilities.

Some of the essential concepts of Bowen theory, however, have been treated cursorily if at all in some of these presentations and books. Especially conspicuous by absence is the concept of differentiation of self, the cornerstone of the theory. Systems thinking, of almost equal importance, is also usually left out of most presentations. Many people, interested in the ideas of Bowen, have asked me for more information about the theory. Specifically, they want to grapple with theory at a more substantive level. They have convinced me that this book would indeed have a place.

The vignettes in this book are not about actual people. Rather, they are composites made up from experiences gained by sitting alongside many real people, observing as they wrestle with life.

Another point is of interest to some. While first names have become commonplace in the therapy world, they are not at Georgetown. Certainly they are never used in presentations. If therapists are addressed by their last names, then it is an invasion of the other's boundary to slide into the informal first name form of address.

I have told my story here in the first person. Many asked that I write the entire book this way. However, in the interest of objectivity, now I would like to get out of the first person. Writing in a relationship style makes contact with people at a certain level. My aim is to define my thinking in the most objective way possible so that theory may become more clear, without the encumbrances to thinking that a relationship poses. There are already several books in print written from that level. They are useful to an enormous number of people. I have found it even more useful to myself and others to aim for a different level, a level that I believe is more conducive to thinking.

Because Bowen family systems theory is a more encompassing way of viewing the human than we have had until now, and considering the depth and breadth of the human problem at this time in history, I believe it is imperative to communicate what is now happening at Georgetown. For me, and for many people I have seen in consultation, beginning to learn to think from a family and natural systems perspective has been more than worth the effort it took and continually takes. Other theories have had far-reaching impacts on the world. It is impossible at this time to predict ways in which Bowen's thinking will impact the future. It is conceivable that the effects will be profound. Much remains to be done. As I see it, we must get on with that work.

This book then is a story about what Dr. Murray Bowen, working on making human behavior into a science, learned about human relationships. It does not have all the answers. But neither is it hackneyed nor trite. It is based on a new theory. It is not a "how to" book except in the sense that theory acts as a guide for thinking one's way out of enigmas. How-to's have but limited application. Theory has universal application; it can point the way in any situation. If people can develop a better way of thinking and find a better way to manage the self, they can solve relationship, or any other problems as they arise.

Roberta Gilbert, M.D.

In Gratitude

A book is the product of many heads and many relationships.

The head of Dr. Murray Bowen speaks for itself throughout these pages. He would not have appreciated embellishment.

The idea for this book sprang from the head of David Gilbert, my brother, in 1986, when he asked me to summarize a paper I had just read at the Georgetown Family Center Symposium. He envisioned a book and was so convinced of the value and need for such a work that he gave me no peace until he could see that I was deep into the project. He, a writer, edited, encouraged, advised, and otherwise moved things along. I appreciate his being there, not only in this project, but in life.

John Byrd, friend and agent, invested a great deal of himself into this book. He carefully edited, enthusiastically shepherded, and patiently taught throughout long crucial phases. His emotional staying power throughout months of rejections from publishers and frustrations with my own limitations has made the difference between the possibility and the reality of a book. Some friends become like family.

Daniel Papero generously and energetically invested many hours and much thinking in this manuscript, right up to the last minute. His great facility with theory as well as with the English language made an invaluable contribution. I am grateful.

Patricia Richter's writing and editing skills made a very positive impact on the manuscript and also on the mind of the author.

Donna Hoel, David Wexler, George Cleveland, Jon Ebersole, and the others at CHRONIMED Publishing have been enthusiastic, responsible, and flexible through all the difficult phases of bringing a good idea into reality.

Mary Bourne lent useful and practical support.

Virginia Earnest, who designed graphics, was competent, resourceful, and a joy to work with.

Readers' invaluable comments have saved the book to such degree as was possible from overadvising, preaching, name-calling, contradicting, help-giving, exaggerating, and theory eroding. Their advocacy in many cases added momentum. They are: Walter Toman, Michael Kerr, Roberta Holt, Kathleen Kerr, Andrea Schara, Priscilla Friesen Felton, Carroll Hoskins Michaels, Donald Shoulberg, Lina Watson, Jennifer Ashby, Louann Stahl, Marcia Macdonald, John Harper, Brad Barr, Richard Jafolla, Mary Alice Jafolla, Anne McKnight, Lee Kelley, Susan Willocks, Lisa Egle, Georgia Jacobs, Victoria Harrison, Frank Giove, Robert Gillanders, Janet Kuhn, LeRoy Bowen, Joanne Bowen, Kathleen Bowen Noer, Morley Segal, Patricia Hyland, and my son, Gregory Jacobs.

A New Way of Thinking About Relationships

A New Way of Thinking About Relationships

I have been thinking theory . . . and working toward a different theory since starting formal family research in 1954. It is not possible to quickly discard one way of thinking and adopt another way of thinking . . . .

Murray Bowen, 1976

It would be difficult to overestimate the importance of human relationships. If love does not make the world go around, then surely relationships do. In the world of the personal, the world of work, and the world at large, relationships between people are a critical and decisive force.

In the realm of the purely personal—after food, water, and shelter—the quality of relationships most often determines the quality of life. In the workplace, the outcome of enterprises often depends on the quality of relationships between people there. Efficiency, productivity, and creativity are the indicators of whether people can balance tasks and relationships. In the community of nations, human relationships start and stop wars.

Contrary to some prevalent notions, smooth-running relationships between individuals—in the family, in the workplace, and even in summit meetings—rarely if ever happen by accident. Rather, those extraordinary relationships that everyone seeks develop over time, when adults relate to each other in principled ways. Few people are aware of what these principles are, however. Furthermore, well-known and widely taught principles can often make things worse.

Often what people accept as ordinary relationships too often are not working very well.

3

Mr. and Mrs. C each had an idea of how relationships should go in terms of housework tasks, finances, and the rearing of their children. Unfortunately, their ideas did not often coincide, and when one of them would disappoint the other, criticism and blame were the order of the day. The fight was on.

Trying to find a way out of this exhausting and fruitless process, Mrs. C read books about marriage, how to fight, and how to communicate. She found rules and techniques that made a lot of sense, and when she could remember to use them, they sometimes worked. In the heat of confrontation, however, she found it nearly impossible to remember these techniques and rules, let alone to use them. Also, some of the advice she found in her books seemed to intensify the fights. She became aware, as she tried out each new idea in turn, that something basic was not being addressed—something she had no way to think about.

The D's avoided criticism and blame like the plague. Theirs was a peace-at-any-price coalition. The cost of not knowing how to address their issues was distance. If disagreement threatened to break out, the subject was changed, or one of them became quiet, unable to think or speak. They really didn't think of this as a problem. It seemed rather a relief from the conflictual homes they had each been exposed to as youngsters. They were aware of relationship discomfort at times, and sometimes they secretly wondered if all marriages were boring and colorless. But they never tried to find a way to change anything.

The O family saw Mrs. O as the problem—if only she were in better health. No expense was spared in her medical treatment, but none of it was effective. Neither the O's nor Mrs. O's many physicians had a way to think about her ill health as a symptom instead of a disease—a symptom of relationship anxiety.

Mr. and Mrs. T didn't fight. They didn't think of their relationship as boring or colorless. Both had excellent health. They did not relate to each other as individuals. They couldn't. Their attention and anxiety were riveted to concerns about someone else. Sometimes it was their children, who did not flourish. Occasionally, one of them became concerned about whether the other was having an affair. They channelled all their relationship anxiety through a third party. Yet, they were not aware that their anxiety, which was considerable, was not really about the third person. It was about their relationship.

These relationship sketches are familiar: Anyone involved in relationships has lived some version of them at one time or another. Many, perhaps most, people experiment with each of them in turn rather than getting stuck indefinitely in any one of them.

Yet, some relationships seem to go very well, with only minimal effort. They seem to flow in a relaxed and enjoyable fashion, neither partner apparently worrying much about it. Such idyllic relationships exist for only a lucky few, no doubt.

More often, relationships between people are delicate and fragile, requiring constant consideration, effort, and a great deal of objectivity. While relationships solve one kind of anxiety—that of being alone—they create another. And for all the investment that goes into them, the returns are often slim. In spite of all the creativity, perseverance, and insight they require, relationships often confound and confuse people. They sometimes end in disappointment and disillusionment.

What is missing in the lives of individuals, families, and corporations when they become bogged down in their relationships? Are there guidelines to help plot a course through the perplexing, precarious domain of relationships? Is it possible to attain the ideal of extraordinary relationships now seemingly reserved for so few?

While there is still much to learn, the family systems theory developed by Dr. Murray Bowen offers some new ways to think about improving one's functioning in important relationships. The principles spelled out in the theory form themselves into a kind of "guidebook." It is currently proving itself to scores of clinicians working with hundreds of people in troubled relationships. These people are able to recognize the freeing aspects of a broader way of seeing. It is this expanded perspective that leads them closer to extraordinary relationships.

DR. BOWEN'S EXTRAORDINARY
WAY OF THINKING

In the early 1950s, many behavioral science researchers wanted to know the cause of the mental illness schizophrenia. This illness typically afflicts young people, leaving them with varying degrees of access to reality. During that time, fortunately, Americans made financial resources available for research in all branches of science, including the behavioral sciences. A new wing at the National Institutes of Mental Health in Bethesda, Maryland, was designated for psychiatric research.

Dr. Murray Bowen came to Maryland fresh from several years of training and practice in the stimulating atmosphere of the Menninger Clinic in Topeka, Kansas. As a resident physician at Menninger, he had realized early on that the predominant theory in psychiatry, Freudian theory, was based on human subjectivity—what patients said and what they and their analysts interpreted it to mean. Bowen believed the study of the human could be made more objective and brought into the realm of accepted science.

Bowen proposed a broader way of thinking about human behavior and a different way of approaching problems. His ideas, if correct, would apply not only to the problem of schizophrenia but to the whole of the human phenomenon. *He had an idea that the basic unit of emotional functioning might not be the individual, as previously thought, but the nuclear family.*

Some researchers in the field had postulated that the mother, by her faulty communication patterns with her offspring, was "the cause" of schizophrenic children's problems. Bowen, too, believed that many human problems were rooted in the family system. But, early on, it became obvious to Bowen that relationship patterns in the families he observed involved not only the mother and the child, but the entire family. While the mother and child were certainly two of the primary players, schizophrenia was not a simple cause-and-effect result of the mother's relationship to her child.

Families were admitted to the NIMH and like ethologist Jane Goodall watching her chimps, Bowen settled in and began to observe the emotional processes at work in the human family.

The relationship patterns in these families were difficult to untangle at first. It was as if individuals were emotionally fused with each other. When one person became emotionally intense, another person would react predictably. These emotional interactions were in constant motion, often taking recognizable forms that, in time, became familiar patterns. Occasionally the staff itself was drawn in.

Moreover, the families of origin of both parents were an important part of the emotional process. They were involved in what Bowen came to see as a multigenerational passing and circuiting of anxiety. Large amounts of family anxiety seemed to focus in one member. Though schizophrenia was considered a disease (a disease that may even have an organic substrate), there was a sense in which it was also a symptom. To some degree, the course of the "illness" was clearly linked to the pervasive family anxiety.

Emotions in the research families reverberated tirelessly from person to person (and even from generation to generation), without resolution. The families seemed to be involved in chronically high levels of self-perpetuating anxiety.

The traditional view of schizophrenia, with mother as cause (the problem) and child as effect (the sick one), was simpler. But Bowen's observations of entire families carved out a new and much broader perspective. The whole family was involved in the emotional process, even though the emotional reactivity between the mother and child was often the most intense and, therefore, the easiest to identify. Bowen realized that if researchers were to adequately describe what they were witnessing, they would have to learn a different way of thinking: "systems thinking."

Systems thinking replaced cause-and-effect thinking. Parents were not causes, but rather were receptors and conduits of, as well as contributors to, a much larger multigenerational emotional process.

This process, while enormously complex, could nonetheless be comprehended to some degree. The emphasis in systems thinking was on seeing the positions of as many of the players on the field (or fields) at one time as possible. And it was a natural system, similar emotionally to groupings in other species.

Bowen soon learned that, if he were to make valid observations, he must himself stay out of the complex and intense emotional patterns of the families he observed. When Bowen and his clinical team were more emotionally calm, the family under observation responded in kind. Under these circumstances everyone in the family made more sense, including the "schizophrenic" child. If, however, Bowen or researchers on his team responded with emotional intensity to the anxiety in the family, everyone's feelings escalated with increased reverberation. When family members were less anxious, they were often able to think through their problems, finding resolution without outside help.

Prevailing theoretical language did not adequately describe these observations. To make sense of them, Bowen drew family diagrams—charts to keep the players straight and reveal important family facts (see Fig. 1). Over time, they would reveal much about family emotions and emotional processes. They also were a way to facilitate systems thinking.

Looking at the functioning and emotional processes of several generations gave a greater understanding of the "big picture" so important to thinking systems.

Therapists learned the unparalleled value of studying the systems and emotional processes of their own families. Bowen could see differences in the functioning of psychiatrists-in-training who worked to change themselves in their own families and those who did not.

Choosing families with schizophrenia for the research turned out to be one of those lucky breaks often encountered in scientific work. The heightened intensity of the emotional processes in these families made the processes themselves more obvious. As the new lens was trained on other families, Bowen confirmed his theoretical observation that emotional processes in the research families differed

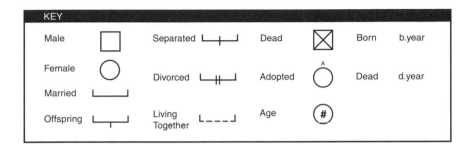

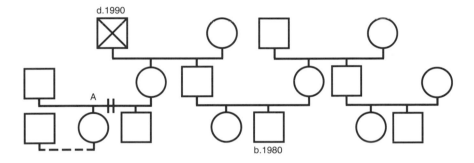

Figure 1. A Family Diagram.—Family diagrams are records of the facts of family history. Birth dates, death dates, locations, moves with dates, education, and health are all recorded on it.

only in degree from those of other families. He saw that families, like individuals, could be arranged on a spectrum of functioning, with some families ranking higher on the scale of functioning and some lower.

To date, although there is a great amount of clinical experience, there is no large body of scientific observation based on Bowen theory. It is only at the first step of a long process that leads to eventual acceptance as fact. It does not claim complete resolution of the complexities of human nature. Nor is the theory primarily a method for practicing psychotherapy. It does not have all the answers for the problems of society. It does, however, provide a framework for expanding understanding in all these areas.

Bowen ultimately developed a theory about human behavior that is comprehensive. Taken in its entirety, Bowen family systems theory opens up a vast new vista on human behavior and human relating that makes older theories seem like looking at the night sky through a knothole in comparison with looking through a telescope.

Bowen's research has shown that certain theoretical principles apply to any human involved in any kind of relationship with another human or humans. The effort to think theory in relationships is what this book is all about. Because of the internal cohesiveness of the theory, study of one part leads naturally and inevitably to the rest. The focus in this book, however, will be primarily on the ideas of the theory essential to a better understanding of human relationships. Only when one has a broader, more effective way of thinking about relationships is there a chance of improving one's functioning in them.

A THEORY ABOUT RELATIONSHIPS

The human has been slow to learn about his own inner space within
his own skull. Thus far we have hardly scratched the surface.

Murray Bowen, 1988

The new way of thinking about the human phenomenon distin-
guishes itself in several significant ways from its predecessor, Freudian theory and its many derivations. One important difference is the
insistence of the new theory upon seeing the big picture. Where
Freudian theory concerned itself with the delineation of ever more
refined detail in the life of an individual, Bowen theory pursues an
ever-broadening scope that incorporates an entire relationship system. Understanding the system and working for personal change
within it produces a powerful effect, not only upon the individual but
on the entire system.

Because psychiatry grew out of the need for medicine to "do
something" about mentally ill persons, it was perhaps inevitable that
the discipline would sustain a symptom-focused point of view. It is
certain that psychiatric research has made headway in both the
diagnosis and treatment of illness. But whenever a focus on symptoms obscures the strengths of people, there may be room for another
approach. Perhaps it will be necessary to dedicate resources to
looking beyond illness or pathology to the discovery of how to make
human life and relationships the best they can possibly be.

A research focus on the understanding of human strengths
instead of on pathology or symptoms is rare. In fact, just as
newspapers rarely print good news, a research focus on the strengths
of human family systems would probably find little support. Yet, if
we are ever to improve the quality of our lives, a model of "the best

11

possible" would be of enormous value. Guiding principles designed to help us reach the ideal would be useful. Bowen family systems theory offers both a clear picture of human potential and a detailed outline of the principles needed to work toward it.

Because all human efforts are profoundly influenced by our thinking, it is important to examine how one thinks about relationships. Moving toward a more objective and inclusive way of thinking makes it possible to see relationships as they really are. To see what they could be, it is important to understand and apply theoretical principles. These principles can help improve relationships.

Learning to think a different way may not be easy. Some describe it as taking off the head and screwing it on an entirely new way. But if one is available for that sort of enterprise, it can be exciting as well as challenging. The first and most important concept in understanding and changing relationships is differentiation of self, which will be described after individuality and togetherness forces. Understanding these forces is basic to understanding differentiation of self.

A second important principle for gaining an understanding of human connectedness is that of emotional systems. Within that concept, *thinking systems* and *observing process* become clear. In the following chapters, these principles will be applied to life situations. But understanding the rest of the book depends on gaining an understanding of these two most important concepts in Bowen theory: The first concerns the self in relationships, and the second, the emotional relationship system in which the self lives.

The Individuality and Togetherness Forces

> The theory postulates two opposing basic life forces. One is a built-in life growth force toward individuality and the differentiation of a separate "self," and the other an equally intense emotional closeness.
>
> **Murray Bowen, 1973**

One of the most fundamental features of the human condition is the struggle that arises out of the need to strike a balance between two basic urges: the drive towards being an individual—one alone, autonomous—and the drive towards being together with others in relationship. Ideally these two tendencies are brought into a fulfilling balance. More often, however, the result is an unremitting tension.

The individuality force pushes toward defining one's self as separate from others. It propels one toward adopting individual beliefs, reasoning out choices, and personal autonomy. This work of building a self, with its beliefs, goals, and boundaries that are distinct from those of other people, begins early in life and, ideally, continues throughout. The individuality force is ever-present in human beings. It reminds one constantly of boundaries that are non-negotiable in our personal relationships.

The togetherness force urges us toward others, for attachment, for affiliation, and for approval. It is an emotional process among individuals in which both anxiety and self are transferred. This movement of emotion and self among individuals is basic to seeing the group as the emotional unit. Looking at nature helps clarify this idea.

In animals, there is a tendency for anxiety to ripple instantaneously through a herd when there is danger. The herd functions as an emotional unit. The anxiety moves from one individual to the next, causing all the individuals to push closer together. The predictable ways in which the group handles anxiety (such as the herd moving closer together) are characteristic of the togetherness force. The force is undoubtedly as old as life itself. Indeed, it is thought that there is undoubtedly a togetherness force that works to direct all aggregates of living cells.

In humans, the togetherness force finds expression in companionship, family, and society itself. In these emotional units, the transfer of anxiety between individuals is such that something of each self is exchanged between them. One person gains and the other loses self as the one viewed as having a problem is focused on by both. Or they can both lose self by focusing on each other or a third.

Togetherness is sometimes called fusion. This refers to the taking on or giving up of self in a relationship. Fusion, or togetherness, is automatic at lower levels of emotional maturity or at any level of maturity when anxiety is running high. While fusion can alleviate anxiety, it can also produce discomfort, and it may consequently push people in the direction of relationship aversion.

The individuality and togetherness forces set up a tension that is a natural and inevitable fact of human life. Their basic, intense, and opposing qualities mean that constant and concerted effort is required in order to keep life in balance.

Is there a proper ratio of individuality to togetherness? Ideally, people at high levels of emotional maturity (differentiation), while they would enjoy relationships, would find little need to complete themselves or route their anxiety through another person. Relationships without togetherness would be comfortable and run smoothly. That is not to say, however, that togetherness is a bad thing. It is an automatic emotional reaction. Automatic emotional reactions are neither bad nor good; they just are. They are simply facts of life.

The more emotionally mature individual finds it easier to manage the individuality/togetherness forces. This person is a more emotionally complete self with less need for attachment to another person. Life is comfortable for this person, whether he or she is in a relationship or alone. The more emotionally mature, or more highly differentiated, person has a greater amount of self with which to negotiate the problems of life, including those of relationships.

At lower levels of emotional maturity, on the other hand, people tend to seek comfort in relationships. They look for someone else to complete the lack of self they find in themselves. They are trying to make a self out of two or more selfs.

In human history, the individuality/togetherness dichotomy can be seen in the contrasts presented by democracy and communism. Democracy emphasizes the rights of the individual, while communism emphasizes the rights of the group. Each society, perhaps as a direct result of its different emphases in resolving the individuality/togetherness problem, may have produced somewhat different problems in its society. Each, as well, may tend to amplify different assets of its people.

Married people sometimes long for the opportunities for fulfillment of the individuality force they fancy present in single life. Single people may long, just as intensely, for the fulfillment of the urge toward togetherness that marriage provides. One's individuality, however, can best be tested in the dual crucibles: by being alone and by being together with others in relationships.

The emotional intensity of a significant relationship is a stimulus that intensifies the drive toward togetherness. As each partner finds personal meaning in the relationship, the togetherness force becomes more intense, as though some sort of gravitational force were operating. The thinking, feeling, and behaving of each becomes "other oriented." The relationship becomes a distraction from individuality (acting, thinking, and feeling as a separate self) and the focus on self is obscured. Once the primary focus is off self and onto someone else, life direction veers off on the course of too much togetherness (the giving up of self into a relationship).

The pull toward togetherness will increase at times of intensified anxiety in the emotional system. For example, it is not uncommon for a marriage to take place soon after the death of an emotionally significant person in a family. Individuality is difficult to maintain and may become easily lost to togetherness. For example, what happens to the ideals of a supposedly solid individual in the midst of his cronies on coffee break? His individuality can be easily surrendered during the telling of a racist joke or gossip in the strong pull of group togetherness.

The state of being alone should not be mistaken for individuality. A well-defined self might be alone, but most often aloneness is probably not an expression of individuality. Rather, more commonly, aloneness is a reaction to intense relationships and the togetherness intrinsic to them.

Togetherness is a function of the extent to which one is not a whole separate self, and the corollary of that idea, the need to complete a self through relationship with another person. These emotional attachment (or togetherness) needs can take many forms.

Attempts to form a self might look like the embattled C family, with each trying to get the other to change into what each thinks is needed; each is preoccupied with the deficiencies of the other, and neither is focused on the self. Another form of togetherness is lived out by the D's who have fused two selfs into one to the degree they become allergic to closeness. The O's togetherness pattern plays out in one of them gaining self in the relationship, with the other losing self into an adaptive position by becoming physically ill.

Mr. and Mrs. T focus on a third person instead of dealing directly with their relationship anxiety, illustrating yet another form togetherness takes. How togetherness plays out is really the story of any life, since all people experience varying amounts of the force, which is constantly present, though it fluctuates in expression over time, depending upon the amount of anxiety in the emotional field.

How do the two forces play out in groups? Most groups trade self among the individuals and, over time, develop relationship patterns that become locked into place. Polarized factions often develop because people are less able to think for themselves, and instead they adopt the views of others automatically. When anxiety runs high in the group, the group makes emotionally based decisions that really amount to nothing more than taking sides. Decisions that are not well thought through stand less chance of being sound over the long term.

By contrast, a group of people, all at high levels of individuality, with less of the togetherness pull, would not be a group at all, at least not in the usual sense. In a high level group, or "collection of individuals," each individual would base his or her thinking and behavior on principle. Each would have an ability to think clearly and calmly to solve problems, and each would define and communicate ideas of their own when appropriate. In the ideal group, cooperation, although evident, would not be based on giving up of self. It would be based on thoughtful examination of issues as they relate to principles and thoughtful conduct of each self in open relationship to other members of the group.

The positions of leader and follower, while clear, in this group of highly differentiated individuals would be less of an issue than is often the case. Each person would act responsibly for self as well as for the life and welfare of the group, as the abilities of each member dictate. Different people might assume leadership roles at different times for different purposes without threatening others or competing with them. Perhaps this sounds like utopia. This kind of interaction among individuals becomes more nearly realized, however, when people begin to interact at higher levels of personal functioning.

The central dilemma in managing the individuality/togetherness force for each person is how to keep the focus on one's own life and life direction but still stay in open, clear communication with the other significant people in that life. Or, stated differently, how can one be the best one can be and still be with others who have that same goal? Bowen theory shows how to head in that direction.

DIFFERENTIATION OF SELF

A graduated scale . . . leads from the total lack of self (undifferentiation), at the lower end, to the total presence of self (differentiation), at the upper end . . . . It is an amazingly accurate concept that describes the factual way an individual is different from all others in the relationship system . . . . On a descriptive level, it is a relationship phenomenon between self and important others.

Murray Bowen, 1988

If any single idea in Bowen family systems theory is central in importance, it is the idea of differentiation of self. It is essential to understanding relationships. Stating the concept simply: *Individuals vary in their ability to adapt—that is, to cope with the demands of life and to reach their goals.*

People range from high levels of differentiation to low levels on a hypothetical scale, depending on how much basic self (the solid part of self that is non-negotiable in relationships) is present (see Fig. 2).

Basic self is "differentiated," or separated, from the emotional system of one's family very early in life, and to different degrees in different people and families. This takes place in the context of mother/child/family togetherness. The degree to which differentiation is set in infancy by the family system may be considerable. Differing degrees of competency have been observed even among newborns. Ideally, at the highest levels of differentiation, one would be a complete and emotionally separate self sometime before leaving one's family of origin.

At higher levels of differentiation, more basic self is present and there is less tendency for attachment of self to others. This is because one is more completely separated emotionally from the original

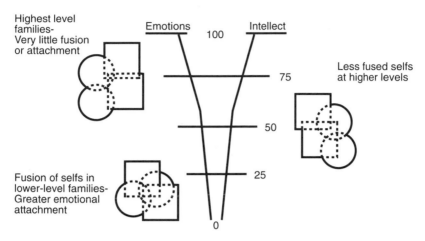

Figure 2. Attachment of selfs at differing levels of differentiation.

family emotional system. Lack of emotional attachment does not imply emotional distance from family members. On the contrary, with less emotional attachment, openness in the emotional system is more characteristic.

Many people reach adulthood without ever developing an ample amount of basic self. This means that, to varying degrees, basic self was only partially formed in their original families. Separation from fusion with others in the family was incomplete. Thus, the self became only partially differentiated. They grew up with other family members always completing them, fused in relationships. Because they separated out less self from the original family emotional system, they act automatically and without being aware of it. In adulthood they tend to try to complete or compensate for the lack in relationships with others. This tendency toward attachment is automatic and outside conscious awareness.

Variation among individuals for adaptation is seen in other species also. Jane Goodall's observations of chimpanzees at Gombe encompass a wide range of adaptation. Her studies show that some are more competent in socially interacting, in rearing their young, and in simply surviving than others. This variation can be seen as different levels of differentiation in that species. One chimp, Flint, and his mother, Flo, were so emotionally attached that Flint's infancy was protracted and he never separated from his mother, staying very near her. When his mother became old and died, Flint, although he was eight and a half years old (an age of independence for most chimps), "fell into a state of grief and depression." He died three and a half weeks after her death in the same spot where she had died.

Sometimes relationships are an attempt to complete the self the same way it was completed in the original family system. There may be a repetition of early patterns, or they may be reacted to and avoided. For example, if primary early relationships were filled with conflict, there may be a tendency to complete the self as an adult by seeking out conflicted relationships. On the other hand, a person may be averse to conflict and try to keep peace at any price in adult relationships.

Human beings will attempt to complete the self in relationships to the degree that it is incomplete by itself. At the same time, the others in their systems will also be aiming for self-completion. The effort to make a complete self out of two undifferentiated selfs results in a fusion of selves. It is based on the need for attachment, or togetherness, that was not resolved in the original family. Fusions, which attempt to pacify the togetherness force, carry with them anxiety of their own that intensifies the relationship. But, if one has developed a more substantial basic self, there is less tendency to compensate for emotional immaturity through fusing with another self.

Two inner guidance systems affect the basic self. One is comprised of the automatic, emotional, or instinctual processes necessary to maintain life. The patterned emotional responses from early life also become part of this automatic guidance system. This system is most likely rooted primarily in the emotional parts of the brain, which are the same as those found in reptiles and other mammals.

The other inner guidance system, which is mostly organized in the cerebral cortex, is newer in evolutionary time. It functions by processes of thought, reasoning, judgment, and logic and has reached its most complex level of development in *Homo sapiens*.

The two together comprise the guidance systems of the self. At higher levels of differentiation of basic self, people have more choice about whether to follow the guidance of the thinking self or the guidance of the emotional/feeling self. They are better able to separate these two functions. At lower levels of differentiation, the intellectual and emotional guidance systems are fused, allowing little or no choice between the two and making the intellect essentially emotionally driven.

Many physical and mental abilities and aptitudes combine in a unique way to form each individual. The inner guidance systems, however, play a major role when it comes to how far one can go with innate abilities and aptitudes. At higher levels of differentiation, the thinking part of the basic self (internal, well thought-out principles and beliefs) is more available and accessible for any purpose, even to modulate and modify emotional reactions, when that is desirable.

How exactly does this work? An individual might have, for example, a large amount of musical talent but not believe it. That belief will limit his or her achievement in music. At the same time, someone else might have a small amount of talent, but believing in his or her gifts, might expand that talent through very hard work into a distinguished musical career. In this way, a person produces repeated failure or success. Well thought-out beliefs about the self, others, and the world, to the extent they are used for guidance, be-come the core of the thinking inner guidance system of the basic self.

At all levels of differentiation, the basic self is surrounded by a greater or lesser amount of functional, or "pseudo," self. The pseudo self can be operating at a higher or lower level of differentiation than the basic self, depending largely on whether external circumstances are adverse or favorable. If external circumstances are favorable, the functional self may operate well, giving the appearance that he or she is a highly differentiated person. If circumstances become adverse, however, and anxiety goes up, this same person may exhibit physical or emotional symptoms or immature behavior.

The functional or pseudo self has more or less permeable boundaries according to the degree of differentiation of self: The higher the differentiation level, the less permeable the boundary. It is the functional part of self that is negotiated when anxiety in the system rises; it is the part that is given up or taken on in relationship fusions with other equally permeable selves. Beliefs that are adopted from the relationship system, rather than reasoned out for the self, become a part of functional or pseudo self.

The basic self needs no support. It is sure, unshakable and non-negotiable. The term "differentiation," properly used, applies only to the basic self and not to the functional self. It is impossible to judge a person's level of differentiation unless observations are made over a long time in many different circumstances. The higher the level of differentiation, the greater the amount of basic self present at all times to guide all behaviors.

The basic self can be thought of as having definite and impermeable boundaries around it. It is neither given up nor taken on in a relationship; there is no borrowing or lending. If the basic self is small, the functional self surrounding it can be thought of as proportionately large, enabling the individual to function in the world.

Thinking, decision making, and behavior originating in the functional self is not optimal. A person with proportionately more functional self has fewer of the benefits of principled inner guidance and will tend to repeat patterns from the past and react to emotional environments more intensely. The better developed (or larger) the basic self, the smaller the functional or pseudo self, and the less permeable (or more intact) the boundaries. Conversely, the less developed (or smaller) the basic self, the larger the functional or pseudo self, and the more permeable (or negotiable) the boundaries (see Fig. 3).

The fact that people at higher levels of differentiation do less trading of self in relationships does not mean they are less cooperative or altruistic. Rather, at higher levels, there is a greater ability for cooperation and altruism. But the cooperation or altruism is accomplished as a thoughtful choice and is guided by inner principles, not as an automatic, adaptive, or accommodative response. Compliance, as well as its opposites, arguing and rebellion, among less differenti-

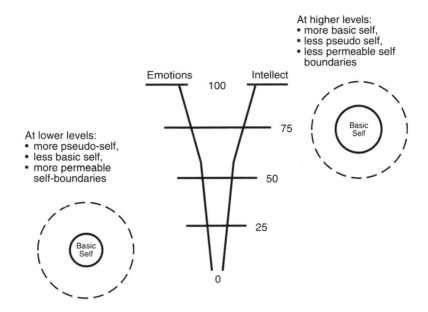

Figure 3.

ated basic selves can be an emotional reaction to the pressure of the group, with negotiation of functional self in an effort to hold anxiety at bay. Giving away or taking on of functional self at lower levels is automatic. In fact, it's nearly reflexive, since it is determined solely by the emotional system.

Since the rational, logical part of the brain does not operate reliably in the presence of strong emotion, people at higher levels of differentiation, based upon a better ability to choose between thinking and feeling, will fare better in the overall management of their lives. Their better ability to make decisions will result in better coping behaviors. They can calm their emotions in order to think their way through difficult situations.

Also, the higher the level of differentiation, the less concern there is about being loved and accepted, or about what others think of one. Living is oriented more around principles, making for smoother relationships, so relationship concerns do not dictate behavior to the same degree they do for those at lower levels. Approaching the problems of life with more ability to call into play a thoughtful inner guidance system results in less anxiety about relationships and all of life (see Fig. 4).

Highly differentiated persons have a superior ability to calm their emotional states, while the less differentiated person can be immobilized by emotion. The highly differentiated person, able to choose emotional states, can thoroughly enjoy them. At the lower end of the scale, however, feelings and the thinking system are intimately connected and there is more anxiety to deal with. Less differentiated families generate more anxiety, both chronic (coming down through generations) and acute (short-term). At higher levels of differentiation of self, there is progressively less anxiety.

In summary, people at lower levels on the scale have difficulty with decision-making; because they have less choice between thinking and feeling, more of their choices are emotionally driven. If they appreciate this fact, they may freeze into indecision when a choice must be made. Their relationships are difficult.

Because of their relative lack of self, those at the lower end of the scale of differentiation are in a constant search to complete a self through fusion with another person. Fusion is an uncomfortable state, however, so relationship well-being is elusive. They have an inordinate concern over being loved and accepted, which may take the form of worrying about what people think of them or the opposite—rebelling against accepted behavior or standards. Either position is anchored in that basic concern for acceptance.

At the lower levels there is a great deal more anxiety on a daily basis. Some of this anxiety is a reaction to outward stresses such as the outcome of bad decisions (acute anxiety). Some is chronic. Originally generated from the family emotional system and years of repetitive patterning, it has become a permanent emotional response of the individual. This chronic and acute anxiety, coming from different sources but experienced as equally negative, has the effect of producing symptoms. The symptoms of anxiety may be emotional, mental, or physical illness or problems, including addictions or rebellious behavior. At the lowest end of the scale, changing the situation is difficult if not impossible.

Most people remain at the level of differentiation attained by the time they left home. However, adults can improve upon that level with hard work. Thinking out one's principles, fundamental to the development of the basic self, is a project everyone can undertake. Improving the ability to choose between thinking and reacting emotionally is possible alone, but a coach or supervisor can greatly enhance one's efforts. Technically, only a small increment of change is possible after leaving one's original family. But any change in the level of differentiation makes for a radical difference in functioning in all areas of life, particularly in relationships.

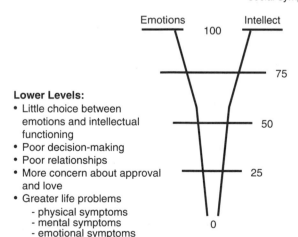

Higher Levels:
- Greater choice between emotions and intellectual functioning
- Better decision-making
- Good relationships
- Less concern for approval and love
- Fewer life problems
    - physical symptoms
    - mental symptoms
    - emotional symptoms
    - social symptoms

Lower Levels:
- Little choice between emotions and intellectual functioning
- Poor decision-making
- Poor relationships
- More concern about approval and love
- Greater life problems
    - physical symptoms
    - mental symptoms
    - emotional symptoms
    - social symptoms

Emotions   Intellect

100

75

50

25

0

Figure 4.

THINKING SYSTEMS, WATCHING PROCESS

This systems theory has made a continuing effort to view man as an evolving integral part of life on earth . . . there is a wide discrepancy between what man does and what man says he does . . . . Systems thinking . . . is directed at getting beyond cause-and-effect thinking and into a systems view of the human phenomenon.

Emotional reactiveness in a family, or other group that lives or works together, goes from one family member to another in a chain reaction pattern.

Murray Bowen, 1973

Until now, therapists and researchers, wanting to know more about how human emotions function, studied the individual. Other people in a family were of interest only as they related to that individual; little attempt was made to understand relationships in the family or how the family worked as an emotional unit or "system."

Bowen theory postulates that the basic emotional unit is the nuclear family. Seen from that perspective, the individual is only a fragment of the emotional unit. In order to understand the individual, the nuclear family must be understood as completely as possible. Emotions are rarely contained within the individual. Rather, they flow endlessly from person to person within the family. Sometimes they spill outside the family to other individuals, family units, or even societal agencies.

"Thinking systems" involves becoming aware of as much of the total relationship system as possible. This includes who the members of the system are, the functional position of each member in it *vis-a-vis* the other, various relationships in it, how emotions are processed through it, and how it all works together to form a system—an emotional unit—as well as how the self fits into the total system.

"Thinking systems" is more than seeing the many ways a person's parents influenced the present adult. If one is merely aware of how various family factors relate to and affect the self, thinking is still running along individual, cause-and-effect lines. If, however, one begins to see how one's parents' relationship affected each of them individually, as well as how it affected one's self, and how their parents and their parents' parents relationships operated—not to mention how one's brothers and sisters, uncles and aunts and cousins fit into the picture and how it all fits together to form a living organism—one is beginning to think systems.

Systems thinking, in Bowen family systems theory, postulates that, as a product of evolution, the emotional part of man's nervous system is more like those of other forms of life than it is different from them. Human relationship systems are a part of all nature, not separate from it. This means emotions are processed within human-relationship systems with an orderliness and predictability similar to that found throughout nature. Although in the past, lip service has been paid to the notion that man is emotionally more similar to, than different from, the rest of the natural world, theories of human behavior have made little use of the idea. Rather, theories have focused on what makes the human being unique—the highly developed cerebral cortex. While theories have not ignored the evolutionarily much older human emotional system, they have shown little appreciation of its connection with the rest of the animal kingdom and little understanding of how, within natural systems, emotionality is connectedness between and among individuals.

With Dr. Paul MacLean's painstaking comparative neuroanatomical studies of "the triune brain," man in his position as part of all nature became clearer. MacLean's work showed that, with evolutionary development, lower functions of the "reptilian" brain (reproduction, aggression) as well as higher "mammalian" brain functions (care and nurturing of the young, audiovocal communication, and play) were preserved intact in the human, with almost unchanged anatomical and functional design.

The distinctive human cerebral cortex came into existence later. It may be less able to influence emotionality than has been previously appreciated. Clinically it seems that in order to change an emotional pattern, the thinking brain must work hard, sometimes for a long time. Also, strong emotion seems to override logical thought; processing information is logically difficult if not impossible during times of heightened emotion.

Actual observations of animal systems by primatologists such as Jane Goodall and Frans deWaal and sociobiologists such as Edward O. Wilson are revealing facts about natural systems that may eventually show that the emotional relationship system of the human and that of other primates hold a great deal in common. Frans de Waal, in his Chimpanzee Politics, says, "If it is hard to explain this . . . social organization without using human terms, it is because we have very similar behind-the-scenes influences in our own society . . . . Our political activity seems to be a part of an evolutionary heritage we share with our close relatives . . . . The roots of politics are older than humanity . . . . My knowledge and experience of chimpanzee behavior has led me to look at humans in another light." Just as ethologists observe animals to learn the facts of their behavior and systems, human family systems thinkers stick to the facts, asking what happened, how, when, where, and to whom. They avoid asking why, which would lead into interpretation and speculation about motivation.

The human dyad is so unstable that when two people who are important to each other develop a problem, which they invariably do, they automatically look around for a third person to include in the anxious situation in some way. The third person is brought into participation in the anxiety of the original twosome, and thus anxiety flows around the triangle.

In any emotional system, a large number of triangles can be observed, with anxiety flowing around them. Human emotional systems are built out of triangles.

Bowen wrote of triangles:

"A two-person emotional system is unstable in that it forms itself into a three-person system or triangle under stress. A system larger than three persons becomes a series of interlocking triangles. The following are some of the characteristics of functioning of a single triangle. As tension mounts in a two-person system, it is usual for one to be more uncomfortable than the other, and for the uncomfortable one to 'triangle in' a third person by telling the second person a story about the triangle[d] one. This relieves the tension between the first two, and shifts the tension between the second and third. A triangle in a state of calm consists of a comfortable twosome and an outsider. The favored position is to be a member of the twosome. If tension arises in the outsider, his next predictable move is to form a twosome with one of the original members of the twosome, leaving the other one as outsider. So the forces within the triangle shift and move from moment to moment and over longer periods. When the triangle is in a state of tension, the outside position is the preferred position, in a posture that says, 'You two fight and leave me out of it.' Add this extra dimension of gaining closeness, or escaping tension, and it provides an even more graphic notion of the shifting forces, each one constantly moving to gain a little more close comfort or to withdraw from tension, with each move by one requiring a compensatory move by another. In a state of tension, when it is not possible for the triangle to conveniently shift the forces within the triangle, two members of the original twosome will find another convenient third person (triangle in another person) and now the emotional forces will run the circuits in this new triangle. The circuits in the former triangle are then quiet but available for reuse at any time. In periods of very high tension, a system will triangle in more and more outsiders. A common example is a family in great stress that uses the triangle system to involve neighbors, schools, police, clinics, and a spectrum of outside people as participants in the family problem. The family thus reduces the tension within the inner family, and it can actually create the situation in which the family tension is being fought out by outside people.

"A triangle characteristically has two positive sides and one negative side. For instance, one member of the close twosome has a positive feeling orientation to the outsider while the other member may feel negative about him . . . . In even the most 'fixed' triangle, the positive and negative forces shift back and forth constantly. A three-person system is one triangle, a four-person system is four primary triangles, a five-person system is nine primary triangles, etc. This progression multiplies rapidly as systems get larger. In addition, there are a variety of secondary triangles when two or more may band together for one corner of a triangle for one emotional issue, while the configuration shifts on another issue."

Many human triangles impinge upon each other, or "interlock." The better this system of interlocking triangles in any emotional system is understood, the better the emotional forces in it are understood. It is impossible to "think systems," therefore, without at least a rudimentary understanding of triangles.

The more one can see the systems-of-triangles perspective, the less prone one will be to take sides, to take things personally, to take thoughtless positions, or to assign blame. When one is thinking systems, one is less prone to adopt the closed-minded position in which one claims to know all the answers, since systems thinking assumes a complexity in reality that is open-ended and always allows for the admission of new data.

In Frans deWaal's descriptions of chimpanzee behavior in the Arnhem Zoo, there are fascinating stories of how three males vied for leadership. The long-term leader, Yeroen, could only be challenged by Nikki or Luit if they could form a coalition between themselves or with powerful female members of the group. The triangles formed during the anxious power struggle were important and endless. Goodall also describes a similar phenomenon in the wild chimpanzees she observes.

Although systems thinking is a more complex way to think, it is highly advantageous. Seen from a broad systems viewpoint, the same situation can often appear very different than it did when seen from either an individual or cause-and-effect thinking perspective.

A systems thinker, able to encompass a great deal of complexity, can easily cut through peripheral nonessentials to the core of an issue. Like the team coach, the musical conductor, or the star athlete who is able to keep in mind the positions of all players at any given time, the systems thinkers learn to consider many parts and their relationships with each other individually as well as with the whole. Thinking natural systems adds an understanding of emotionality that can be gained in no other way.

The ability to see not only one's own position but also the position of the other and how the two fit together enables one to conduct one's part of the relationship better. When two people are in a meaningful relationship, they bring to it their contexts in other systems, such as their extended family or their workplace. If one can understand the other's systems and his or her contexts in his or her systems more fully, one's viewpoint will, by definition, have enlarged.

People can learn to think systems, but it does not come naturally to most. Opportunities for practicing systems thinking are everywhere—at the workplace, a sporting event, a concert. At work, relationships can sometimes be seen more objectively, with greater clarity, than they can in the more primary relationships at home. Taking the next step to see how those relationships affect each other—that is, how relationships fit into triangles of a larger system—can be intriguing.

When Mr. U, who was addicted to alcohol, tried to understand his relationship with his mother by looking only at that relationship, he made very little progress at getting beyond his lifelong pattern of assigning blame. When he took a look at the triangle formed by himself, his mother, and his father, he could see the patterned flow of anxiety in it: his mother's anxious focus because he was the youngest child (youngests in her family had not done very well) and his father's intensity in response to her anxiety. His father wanted to fix things so she would not be anxious, and he became angry at the young Mr.

U when her anxiety continued. Mr. U could see himself assume a frozen, "shut-down" posture when he was the focus of his parents' anxiety. Seeing the posture for what it was—a reaction to the flow of anxiety—he found some new options in managing himself. Shortly after he identified anxiety in patterns in his parental triangle, Mr. U could also see how that triangle was connected to other triangles in the family system, connected by emotional intensity in fairly predictable patterns.

In observing, the focus is not only on the architecture of the system (the triangles and how they interlock), but on the actual movement of anxiety within that system of triangles. "Watching for process" is observing how emotions flow and change within and among the individuals and triangles of a relationship system.

Most lives are filled with dilemmas demanding answers, problems requiring solutions. As a consequence, most people seem to spend a great deal of time in pursuit of answers and solutions. Relationships, too, run into dilemmas involving issues, and partners can get lost in this same pursuit for answers. People can become completely absorbed in an effort to find out how to resolve their differences or how to make someone else behave according to expectations. Although this focus on content is understandable, given the challenges with which life is filled, and the automatic nature of that response, there is an alternative way to think about the functioning of relationships. If one can focus on and manage emotional process better, one is better able to resolve the issues.

An important part of thinking systems is an ability to see emotional process within the system one is observing. In order to see the functional positions of people in the system more clearly, it is useful to watch for emotional process in the system—to observe the facts of how, when, and under what conditions who does what. Seeing the emotional process in relationship systems, then, has to do with watching the inexorable movement of anxiety through the system, over time, as the principals play out togetherness.

The period of observing may be brief—maybe less than a minute. It doesn't take long to observe a glance and someone else's reaction to that glance. Or a process may be observed over years, lifetimes, or generations, as is often the case when studying one's own family system. Whenever the focus can be lifted from the issues, however briefly, a great deal will be learned, and "solutions" brought that much closer. In other words, the solution to most problems, especially when one is stuck, has as much to do with how one goes about the problem-solving process as it does with the actual content of the problem.

When watching for process, thoughts, feelings, and behavior must all be monitored if all parts of the process are to be included. Seeing the behavior of the principals and how they posture themselves toward one another over time will also involve seeing how these postures are affected by anxiety, as well as by all the other members of the relationship system.

Watching for process is complex but fascinating. It involves watching for as many parameters and patterns of functioning of the self and others in the system as possible—over as much time as possible. If one continues to watch emotions moving through a group of people, staying emotionally uninvolved, one has already learned something about managing oneself emotionally. As one observes thoughts, feelings, and behavior as they move in a group of related people, and even within the self, one can often see repetitions. For example, if every time anxiety rises one becomes critical, a tendency to criticize can be used as a marker of intensifying anxiety. This enhances the ability to watch for the process behind that anxiety so it can be managed better.

Mrs. A became aware of a family pattern that was as old as she could remember when she forced herself, after a long-standing cut-off, to visit her home. At the dinner table, Mrs. A's father would invariably find something about her mother to criticize. Her mother would look sad and depressed. Predictably, Mrs. A would jump in and defend her mother in some way. After learning all this by simply remaining emotionally quiet and observing, she was able to sit all the way through a family dinner without criticizing or defending anyone, seeing it instead as their problem. At this point, seeing the family emotional process clearer, she knew she was a little more "out" of it.

The ability to watch for process implies, and will promote, the development of an advancing degree of competence in the management of the emotional part of the self. This is because, in order to observe emotional process, it is necessary to stay emotionally calm. Watching emotional process requires the detached focus of a scientist; the moment one's emotions intensify, one sees less clearly. Since emotional reactivity is infectious, it requires self-discipline to watch emotional process calmly and not become emotionally aroused. And like any new skill, the more one works at it, the more adept one becomes. In time, as the ability to see process as well as issues improves, the ability to manage one's own emotions is strengthened.

RELATIONSHIP PATTERNS AND POSTURES

> The level of differentiation of self determines the degree of emotional fusion in spouses. The way the spouses handle the fusion governs the areas in which the undifferentiation will be absorbed and the areas in which symptoms will be expressed under stress.
>
> **Murray Bowen, 1972**

Relationship difficulties seem, at least to the clinical consultant, to be the rule in human interactions rather than the exception. The following generic relationship story line could serve as a formula for many books. It's also, unfortunately, the bread and butter of the clinician.

Two people meet. They are attracted. They begin to see each other frequently. They talk a great deal, sharing reams of personal history. Their attraction grows into intensely positive feelings generated whenever they are together. After a while, the feelings are aroused just by the thought of each other.

They fuse, emotionally, two selves into one. A symptom of that fusion is the ability of one person to stimulate, or trigger, the other emotionally. If one is happy, the other is happy. If one is sad, the other is sad. More specifically, if one is intense emotionally, the other becomes intense. Sometimes intense elation or sadness in one can trigger anger or frustration in the other.

Shortly after the initial stage, they notice that negative feelings are sometimes generated. These negative feelings can range from a vague anxiety having something to do with the relationship to extreme feelings of threat, insecurity, or jealousy. In the beginning, these negative feelings are brief, although often they seem to take over the relationship fairly rapidly. In time, there is more anxiety than positive feeling.

The two begin to wonder what good the relationship is. They stay together, partly because they are able to generate the good feelings periodically—often enough to give them hope for the future of the relationship. Or they may stay together only because of such extra-relationship considerations as money or children. Sometimes just the memory of their initial attraction is enough to keep them together.

Having gone through this wearisome cycle several times, some finally lose faith in the possibility of durable, satisfying relationships. Where does one begin to make it better? That is the pressing question of most people who seek professional help for personal problems. Clinicians routinely see spouses who have separated from each other but remain as unhappy apart as they were together. They see people who fear being fired if they can't get along with their coworkers better. Or they see parents who become extremely agitated over their relationships with their children. Unfortunately, when faced with relationship problems, most people do not know how to make the fundamental change that is called for. *Usually what people do in a relationship crisis is more of the same thing they have been doing, only more intensely and more anxiously.*

When anxiety decreases sufficiently, people can begin to think about their problems. Anxiety impairs the ability to think. A thoughtful approach usually reveals that the partners are in a relationship pattern that, though not serving them well, is not new. It may have begun years ago; it may even go back to childhood or previous generations. What is important is that people be able to see patterns of thoughts, feelings, and behaviors where they exist. Once they can objectively see the pattern and how it repeats itself over time, they are in a position to see their own contribution to it.

One's own part of the relationship pattern is the only part that one has the power to change. But just as it takes two to make a fight, it takes two (or more) to make any of the relationship patterns. For example, if one of the persons in a relationship has troublesome physical, mental, or emotional symptoms, these symptoms are often seen as the problem of that one alone. More often, the symptoms are merely the expression of anxiety in the relationship. In reality, each person plays a part in producing the symptoms, so if one person changes his or her contribution to the relationship problem (without leaving), the whole pattern will often change.

It is useful to try to understand as much as one can about the pattern—how it developed and what currently triggers it. But the hard work of changing it is a solitary effort. That work begins, proceeds, and ends with a great deal of thought. Thinking is required to understand the pattern, how family patterns enter into it, what one's own contribution to the pattern is, and how to change that. Practice is required, too. One's own part in relationship patterns, learned by watching objectively, can always be improved by patient trial and error.

To start thinking about relationships as patterns, it is useful to consider in some detail the elements of patterns: feelings and emotional reactivity.

EMOTIONS IN RELATIONSHIPS

The scientific facts of evolution have been chosen to replace many of
the ideas of Freudian theory. Evolution is a rich body of facts that can
be proven and validated.

Murray Bowen, 1988

Who would want to live without feelings? They bring with them
color, energy, and momentum. Emotions are important to all life,
firing the strong, quick reactions necessary to survive the dangers of
existence. They make possible procreation and rearing of the young,
insuring the continuation of the species. Nest-building instincts,
territoriality, and play are also an indispensable part of the natural
order. Feelings color life with fun, acceptance, and warmth.

Emotions are the intense reactivities, both physiological and
mental, including the instincts, that are generated in the part of the
brain humans share, anatomically and functionally, with the rest of
the animal kingdom. They are highly complex behavior patterns that
are so necessary to the survival of both the individual and the species
that nature has given them an insistent quality and hard-wired them
into the nervous system. They include such activities as warding off
danger, establishing territory, procreation, and nurturance of the
next generation. Although the functioning of basic emotional/instinc-
tual behaviors may become impaired as a result of anxiety or illness,
their hard-wiring and insistent quality make it difficult to access them
for change voluntarily. They can sometimes be so strong they seem to
carry with them life and death urgencies.

Emotions often are patterns that became established early in
one's personal history, and these patterns may or may not be relevant
to the present. For example, a person who was reared by a father who

beat him or her after raising his voice may be triggered into extremely intense life-and-death emotions whenever he or she is around people who raise their voices. Although this reaction is inappropriate to adult life when no abuse or threat is present, the pattern became part of the emotional repertoire of the nervous system early on.

Positive emotional patterns are likewise set up in the nervous system. For example, the aroma of pine trees, a smiling face, or the smell of turkey cooking in an oven may all be part of pleasurable patterns preserved in the brain from one's personal history in the same way.

Somewhat distinct from emotions are "feelings," which are simply emotions that have come into awareness. Feelings and emotions can be triggered by all sorts of situations and perceptions, whether or not they reflect basic life instincts.

While they are necessary, desirable, and pleasurable, feelings and emotions also lead to most of the difficulties in relationships. In fact, emotional intensity and feelings can wreak havoc in relationships, partly because so many hard-wired emotional patterns are counterproductive to relationships. For reasons unknown, relationships by nature strain and bend under the influence of strong feelings. Although relationships automatically elicit strong feelings in most people, these same strong feelings also play a role in doing those relationships in.

It is not necessary to label and qualify all the different kinds of feelings that exist in human life. The diagnosis and description of subtle and even obvious differences can lead to a focus on pathology, which then becomes an end in itself. Diagnosing pathology doesn't change anything. If one thinks, instead, in general terms of the emotional intensity or "anxiety" that exists in a system, time and energy are freed to think about options for managing it. Emotional intensity or "anxiety," whatever its exact expression (whether depression, anger, or even excessive elation), while providing some of the highs of relationships, also interferes with people's ability to relate to each other optimally.

Anxiety, of course, is part and parcel of the human condition: There is no escaping it. Since anxiety is a powerful teacher, it is doubtful that anyone would want to live a totally anxiety-free life. Anxiety can be acute (short-term), as in a crisis, or it can be chronic, lasting many years or even generations.

In difficult relationships, there is a reverberation of emotion from person to person that is very much like the excitement that begins with one animal and spreads through the entire herd. It is almost as if, in relationship systems, electrical connections link the individuals of the system, transporting emotions and feelings from one individual to another continuously.

Emotional reactivity passes like a hot potato between individuals. When one anxious individual succeeds in exciting a second, the first is often relieved. In humans, this phenomenon results in nothing ever getting resolved. The problem that triggered the emotions is never addressed; emotions are merely generated and then circuited and recircuited through the system. This tendency of emotions to pass in patterned ways from one individual to another, in a family or group of individuals who are significant to each other, is a tendency of the nuclear family emotional process, sometimes referred to simply as the emotional process.

The lower the overall level of differentiation in the relationship system, the more this passing of emotions occurs. Emotionally mature (highly differentiated) individuals seem able to absorb a large amount of stress or be around other excited individuals without themselves becoming emotionally excited or passing it on. This is part of what is meant by having more choice about being in emotions or in thinking.

Less mature (or less differentiated) individuals, however, handle themselves emotionally quite differently. Their relationships are susceptible to a great deal of mutual emotional stimulation, partly because there is a great deal of trading of selves involved. That is, the relationship itself serves the emotional purposes of the selves; the relationship provides emotional stimulation, motivation, support, or other qualities lacking in each partner. It may provide a way of dealing with anxiety, for example, if one uses one's partner for the unloading of anxious feelings.

In time, however, borrowing and lending of selves becomes a source of stress. Since trying to make a self out of a relationship cannot work, the attempt itself creates a certain amount of anxiety. *In order to manage that anxiety, partners begin to posture themselves in recognizable ways, and certain well-known relationship patterns form.*

The five familiar and well-defined relationship patterns, as described by Bowen, are:

- Conflict

- Distance

- Cutoff

- Dysfunctional spouse (also called overfunctioning/ underfunctioning reciprocity)

- Dysfunctional child (also called triangling)

These patterns form to "solve" the problem of relationship anxiety. The basic problem, emotional immaturity, does not get addressed. The same emotional immaturity that led to the attempt to complete a self through affiliation with another self in the first place is merely played out in the relationship pattern. It then becomes clear that emotional immaturity, pushed into a relationship, becomes a burden on that relationship.

Patterns may intensify over time. This is because when things are not going well, the human tends to redouble efforts rather than change the quality of the process. A couple involved in the distance pattern may intensify its distance to the point of cutoff in divorce.

If two partners in a relationship work on their own levels of differentiation, their relationship will automatically improve. If even one of the partners works to raise his or her level of differentiation, the relationship will do better over the long term. This is because, in time, the other partner will almost always raise his or her level also. A person cannot change his or her half of the relationship problem without changing the relationship fundamentally.

Now, for a closer look at each of the relationship patterns.

CONFLICT

> The basic pattern in conflictual marriages is one in which neither gives in to the other or in which neither is capable of an adaptive role. . . . The relationship cycles through periods of intense closeness, conflict that provides a period of emotional distance, and making up, which starts another cycle of intense closeness.
>
> **Murray Bowen, 1976**

A conversation with partners of a conflicted relationship often sounds like this one, with the C family.

Consultant: What's been happening since we met last?

Mrs. C: We have been on vacation, except it wasn't any vacation.

Consultant: Care to say more about that?

Mrs. C: It was just constant fighting, bickering, and arguing, Just like we always have, and I am beginning to think, always will.

Consultant: What seemed to trigger your difficulties this time?

Mrs. C: No matter what I did or said, he would criticize me. I can't seem to do anything right. I never seem to be able to make him happy no matter what I do and, frankly, I'm really tired of trying. I think he is just an unhappy person and is probably going to remain unhappy. Whatever I suggested on the vacation, places to go or places to eat, he would find fault with everything, including me, myself. I don't think we have anything in common. This is the worst marriage

I have ever seen anyone have and why we stay together is more than I can tell you.

Consultant: I would like to hear what was going on in your head, Mr. C, while your wife was speaking.

Mr. C: She's right. We did have a lot of difficulties on our vacation. I don't think I feel quite that hopeless about our situation, but we did argue and fight a lot.

Consultant: Any ideas about what is triggering your difficulties lately?

Mr. C: I just can't handle her ups and downs. Either she's on Cloud Nine or she's in the depths of anger and depression. I don't know how to handle her moods. I can't get close to her, no matter what I try. It's like she doesn't want to be close. She accuses me of being unhappy. She is the one who seems like an unhappy person to me. I don't even have much desire to be close to her anymore. We had one of the worst blow-ups we've ever had about the fifth night of our vacation. That ruined the whole trip for me. The rest of the time it was mostly just petty fighting and bickering, day after day. When she wasn't planning our whole day down to the last minute, she was threatening to get on a plane and come home early without me. I really don't know why I stay around.

Consultant: Mr. C, would you have any idea at all about what your contribution to getting or keeping these things going might be?

Mr. C: Doctor, I really don't feel it's my problem. I think I'm just tied up with a disagreeable, unhappy person who has deep-seated problems. I feel she is the one who needs the help. I honestly don't feel I contribute to the fighting that goes on between us. I have good relationships at the office, with the kids, and with my own family.

She's the only one I absolutely cannot get along with. No matter what I buy her or how I change, she complains and bitches, moans, and groans.

Consultant: *It would seem that it might take two to make a fight or an argument, Mr. C.*

Mr. C: *You would think so, but I have changed a great deal. I am really quite easy to live with. Joan refuses to change at all, and I'm getting very tired of it.*

Consultant: *Mrs. C, what are you thinking of the conversation your husband and I are having?*

Mrs. C: *It's no different than it ever has been. I think I've made a lot of changes as a result of all the books I have read, but all I ever get from Bill is criticism and put-downs. I can't understand why he can't see what he is doing to me. He really doesn't seem to care.*

These two people are locked in a pattern of emotional ping-pong typical of relationships in conflict. Partners in opposition follow a dramatic course, which inevitably and repeatedly seems to butt them up against each other. They are caught in a war of invective, accusation, and competitive escalation. The pain of their relationship seems to well up and spill out from them, poisoning their environment with distressing regularity. Conflictual partners often deliberately avoid other people, fearing their conflict might embarrass them. Paradoxically, between episodes of conflict, they often enjoy a gratifying closeness.

At times of greatest intensity, their relationship may be punctuated by episodes of physical abuse. Theirs is a gut-wrenching, lonely life. Other people, observing the chronic nature of their problem, may come to the conclusion that they enjoy this state of affairs. Actually, nothing could be further from the truth. They are intensely aware of their pain. Of all the relationship patterns, people caught in conflict are most apt to seek help because of their awareness of pain.

Conflicted relationships can be diagrammed like this:

Figure 5.

Although they tend to blame their current partner for their problems, people who are involved in conflicted relationships may be no strangers to conflict. They may have grown up with it. Sometimes conflicted relationship partners grew up, not with conflict, but with other patterns that were just as difficult. It is not necessary to learn conflict (or any other pattern), however. They are automatic, given triggering circumstances. Jane Goodall found that conflict and violence among the chimps she observed was greatly increased when their territory was shrunk by development. Presumably, under these conditions, the anxiety of the animals increased.

Like the other patterned ways of relating, conflict is merely a way of handling relationship anxiety. Sometimes the anxiety does not stem from the relationship; anxiety of any type can trigger conflict. Often when asked what triggered a fight, one partner will answer, "I think I was just trying to pick a fight. I could feel it coming on. It was as though I had to." Conflict becomes more intense at times of increased anxiety, just as do any of the relationship patterns.

People in conflict characteristically show tendencies to:

- become critical when anxiety is high,
- become embroiled in blame for perceived problems,
- project their own problems on other people,
- focus more on the other than on the self,
- fight rather than switch, have fun, or do anything useful,
- behave abusively.

How is it possible to change a pattern of conflict? Usually people are told if they will only get their feelings out, the conflict will disappear. Unhappily, many who take this advice find that the more they try to get their feelings out, the worse the conflict becomes. Also, they find the other person really doesn't care to hear a recital of their feelings.

Another recommendation to conflicted partners is to learn to fight fairly. Sometimes lists of rules are given for doing this. When a fair fight is described, however, it sounds very much like a reasonable conversation and not at all like a fight. Unfortunately, partners in a conflicted relationship are completely unable to get from where they are to any kind of rational involvement with one another, even with lists of rules.

With only a little reflection, an objective observer of Mr. and Mrs. C would rapidly come to the conclusion that if each partner would stop focusing on the other and begin focusing on *self* and the contribution of *self* to the problem, the first step to solving the problem would be behind them. As therapists watch conflicted people, they often think, "If only one of the two could calm down!" And this is true: If one of two conflicted parties in a relationship could learn to remain calm and thoughtful in the face of the anxiety of the other, there would be no conflict. It actually does take two to make a fight.

But how does one remain calm and thoughtful in the presence of an anxious other who wants to fight? When emotion threatens to take over, one can look for principles to show a way out. In the case of the C's, when Mr. C was able to step out of the conflict mentally and watch it quietly for a while, his emotional response calmed to the extent he could see his own part in the fight. At that point, he was able to stop making accusations, listen to what his wife was saying, and represent himself in a more reasoned way.

"Thinking systems" enabled him to remember the conflictual marriage of his parents. Many times he had vowed that his marriage would be different. And yet, here he was, in a relationship posture similar in many ways to that of his parents. Thinking systems enabled him to see how the emotional patterns in his family of origin had, over time, become a part of his own personal emotional system, a system wired into him. That broader view is sometimes used by people to criticize their background. Mr. C used it to see that, although conflict was an emotional pattern he was used to, he had other choices in responding to anxiety.

Another way of thinking systems was for Mr. C to look at a bigger picture, to adopt a broader outlook on his immediate situation. For example, on their next vacation, when small issues threatened to erupt into conflict, Mr. C was able to put them in perspective by mentally removing himself from the anxiety generated by the relationship. He then placed himself in the context of being on vacation. Keeping in mind the systems of people around him—their work systems, their families, their community circumstances—he became fascinated by the place he was visiting. His stay with his wife, put into a systems context, turned every happening into an adventure and brought a movie-like quality to the vacation, with Mr. and Mrs. C as the stars.

Mr. C thought of the scale of differentiation of self—the range of adaptability that exists among people. This principle reminded him he had a choice between feeling and thinking, that he might be losing self in the relationship, and that in a spectrum of possible responses, some of his own might be less mature, less thoughtful, and more emotionally reactive than he would like. So he began to formulate in his mind what, on the scale of differentiation, a higher level, less reactive response might be. He could see he had been repeating his old immature behavior patterns. When he felt anxious, he would usually find someone to blame. Something about being in a fight had previously had the effect of calming him. Also, he usually won the fights; winning somehow bolstered his self-esteem. Working toward differentiation would mean finding new ways of thinking about himself and of calming his anxiety. When his wife started the conflict, he fought back, as if by reflex. Differentiating a self from the family system he and Mrs. C had created meant he would have to find a way to stay calm when she was upset and continue listening to and talking with her. Differentiation of self has everything to do with improving one's own emotional functioning. It has nothing to do with changing the other, so Mr. C had to learn to stay on track with himself. He had to learn to suspend all criticism, censure, and challenge and attempt always only to manage himself better emotionally.

The task of changing a conflictual relationship into a more smoothly functioning one might seem impossible. One or both people sometimes have had years of involvement in, or exposure to, conflictual relationships. Since patterns are highly resistant to change, Bowen experimented with a radical idea. He asked people to take their patterns back into the family system in which the pattern developed in the first place—the family of origin. Often, that effort produced more worthwhile results toward differentiation of self than efforts within the present primary relationship system. The results are obtained by not trying to change the people in the family, but by attending to one's own reactions and ways of relating to the people in the extended family system.

Mr. C worked on changing his own emotional patterns within his family of origin by visiting his family more often. He also called and wrote more often. In the beginning, it was automatic for him to react emotionally when his parents began to fight. After gaining some skill at watching that pattern within himself, he was able to observe their intense behaviors without taking part in them. Later, he was able to talk calmly and thoughtfully to them, whether or not they were in a fight. This work took place over several years and demanded much thought and effort. But over time, all of Mr. C's relationships changed as he learned to manage himself emotionally around his parents. He stopped blaming. His temper, which had always been a problem, decreased. His relationship with his wife became calmer and more thoughtful, as well as more fun.

When a fight or argument is brewing, what can one do about it? What can be done or said outside of the usual pattern? Just watching the process is itself calming. Calm, thoughtful, careful watching can often teach one what is needed to make significant changes in one's own part of the relationship pattern.

The goal of decreasing one's reactivity to the other's emotions is often perceived as distancing oneself from the other person. *But distance is itself an emotionally patterned reaction.* If one leaves the scene or stops one's half of the conversation, that too is emotional intensity. The goal is not to react as emotionally intensely and to continue to stay in calm communication with the other person. This is not easy to attain, but simply having it in mind is useful.

DISTANCE

There is a spectrum of ways spouses deal with fusion symptoms. The most universal mechanism is emotional distance from each other. It is present in all marriages to some degree, and in a high percentage of marriages to a major degree.

Murray Bowen, 1976

The D's had been on vacation, too. They were in the Bahamas attending a professional meeting. Lying on the beach, her eyes focused on the sparkling waves, Mrs. D was deep in thought. She and her husband had a good life. They had few financial worries. Mr. D had done very well with his firm and, in a few years, he would retire. Mrs. D had been primarily responsible for rearing the children. Mr. D was relatively uninvolved with that, especially in the early years, since his job had required him to travel a great deal. At times, Mrs. D wished he could have been more involved with the children's growing up. It seemed that the crises always occurred when he was out of town, but she learned to cope and actually became quite proud of her ability to manage whatever came up. But now the children were grown, and they were, on the whole, doing pretty well.

Unlike some of their friends, the D's relationship had survived their children's teenage years. This thought cheered Mrs. D during times when her anxiety would get focused on her relationship with her husband. Sometimes, however, she found herself wondering what she would do with him under foot all day long after his retirement. What would they have to say to each other? He had been absent so much through the years that she wondered if they really knew each other now. Would they perhaps tire of each other, once they were together more? Her thoughts were interrupted abruptly as her husband shook cold droplets of water all over her after his swim in the ocean. They laughed, exchanged small talk, and after a while, went to the beach bar for a drink.

Later, while he napped, she walked the beach alone. Again, she thought about their relationship. She could not shake the nagging idea that perhaps she was dreading his retirement, dreading having him around. As she followed this line of thought, she started to feel terribly guilty.

That evening, they ate lobster, danced to the island musicians, and chatted with each other and with other couples they met. Mrs. D never seemed to find a time to talk about her concerns. They seemed so negative, she feared they would ruin a good time. Then, a comedian started a very salty routine about love-making in the sand. Eventually, they walked back to their cottage and made love. Life seemed pretty good. Mrs. D didn't fall asleep right away but instead lay awake wondering why she and her husband never talked about anything really important. She fell asleep, as she often did, wondering and worrying.

The next day she began to think about all the parts of life they had never shared. During the early years of their marriage, Mr. D was gone often and she was alone with the kids. His domain was work: making and managing their money. She had no idea what their financial position was and, if she ever had to, would have no idea how to cope with finances. She had once tried to talk with him about this, but all he would say was, "Don't worry about it."

Did he fear thinking about his own mortality, or did he just dislike discussing finances with her? Why was it so hard for them to get beneath superficialities? She tried to think of ways to get through to him to ask her questions and express her concerns. Perhaps he would listen to her if she were more intense, pleading, or assertive. Perhaps, if she showed him more attention, he would make more contact with her.

When they returned home, she tried all those things. None of them worked very well. The more she tried, the less he seemed to care.

The more she pushed for answers, the less he was actually home. It was golf, cards with friends, or a trip out of town. They didn't talk about anything important. The distance was a pattern—an unspoken, unwritten rule by which they lived.

This posture of distance is difficult to think about. Part of the difficulty is that people often equate it with the idea of giving each other "space," or relieving togetherness tensions. Recognizing the fusion of selves in their relationship, people often opt for distance and call it individuality. Even in the best relationships, periodic distance, or at the least apartness, plays a modulating role. To confound matters further, it is possible to see distance in all the other relationship postures, see it as the basic relationship problem, and conclude the other relationship postures are only an outgrowth of the basic distance stance.

The story of the couple above is seen often enough clinically, however, to warrant definition and description of distance as a pattern distinct from the others. The meaningless aloofness seen in the distanced relationship stands in sharp contrast to the intense involvement seen in the conflictual one. Distance is a relationship pattern so common that it is often not seen as a problem. While the participants experience inner pain of sometimes great magnitude, they tend to deny their pain, seeing their distanced position as normal.

Distancing may take several forms, so there are several ways to diagram distance. One partner may distance in response to the other partner's pursuit. The more partner A pursues, the more B distances, which elicits more pursuit in A, and on and on.

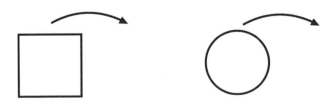

Figure 6A. **The pursuit-distance form of distance.**

Or they may both be distancing overtly.

Figure 6B. Both partners are distancing overtly.

Another way to diagram distancing, which emphasizes the intensity leading to it, is by showing several lines of intensity cut off by the distance.

Figure 6C. Distancing, another form of emotional intensity.

Although one partner may be seen as "the distancer," both parties, as in any relationship pattern, play their parts in it. If the pattern is one of pursuit and flight, the pursuer plays his or her part just as surely as does the fleeing partner. Although the pursuer may complain long and loud about "the distancer," the pursuer is making his or her own contribution to keeping the distancing pattern in place. The flight may be a response to being pursued, in which case distancing may be resolved if pursuing can be stopped or calmed down.

The distance relationship pattern can give rise to other problems. Often a person whose partner is distancing can become very jealous, convinced there is a triangle or he or she is unloved. If one partner distances into work, the other may actually become jealous of the work situation, which can come to be seen as the problem.

Distancing partners often take refuge in overwork, substance abuse, or jobs requiring travel. (However, all people in careers involving travel are not in distant relationships.) Ultimate forms of distance are cutoff, divorce, or suicide.

Signs of distancing include:
- excessive periods of noncommunication when one is emotionally reactive
- workaholism
- overuse of substances such as alcohol
- excessive time spent on hobbies
- a tendency to be quiet when anxiety rises
- talk that includes nothing of personal importance
- an inability to relate to some of the people in one's immediate or original family

People who are involved in a distant relationship often see their part in it as an attempt to help the relationship—to give it some breathing room. Or there may be a manipulative use of distance, in an attempt to draw the other in. Sometimes distance is an attempt to get far enough away from the troublesome relationship to gain control of one's own emotions again. Distancing partners may not trust themselves to relate to each other at all until the intensity abates. Often a distancing partner is playing out an old response to emotional intensity within the self or guarding against the possibility of conflict, as experienced in the family of origin. Most commonly, distancing seems to be an automatic attempt to make the relationship tolerable by getting periodic relief from its emotional intensity.

Unfortunately, the attempt to make things better for oneself or the relationship through distancing is rarely successful. Outwardly the partners express distance towards each other, but inwardly they maintain an intense focus on one another and the relationship. Distance can provide some temporary emotional calm, but over time distancing actually intensifies feelings.

As with conflicted relationships, people involved in distancing often can find this posture in many relationships in their families of origin. They may have had (and have) only superficial or meaningless relationships with their siblings. Or they may have grown up with a distant posture between their parents. Often the pattern can be seen in many generations of a family.

How does one begin to think about a distant relationship? If one can step back and take a good long look at the relationship over time, one can usually learn a great deal. How does the pattern emerge out of anxiety? How effective is it at managing anxiety? How much does it contribute to it? When Mrs. D took an objective look, she realized the chronic distance pattern in her marriage had generated more anxiety than it had calmed. She had no idea how it actually began, but she knew that for many years the distant pattern of her marriage did not seem like a problem. It seemed preferable to the conflict of her parents.

In time, however, she wanted to make meaningful contact in her relationship. She could see that when making contact around important issues became a priority, the relationship pattern changed. At a point when anxiety became especially intense for her, Mrs. D did what is often advocated as a way of managing feelings: She told her mate about them with a great deal of feeling. The more her feelings spilled out to her husband, the more he would distance. As the process of their pattern became clearer, she was better able to see what her part in the distance was. As she began to see how others, especially her husband, reacted to her intense way of presenting herself, she realized there might be other ways to approach him.

Her work had just begun. A great deal of practice is required before any new behaviors become part of the working emotional repertoire. When they do, one has pushed one's level of differentiation of self up to a higher level.

Gaining objectivity about one's relationship stances certainly involves thinking systems and gaining as much understanding of those systems as possible. The effort involves asking many hard questions: "How do I distance from my extended family?" "How do people in my family distance from each other?" "How many distant relationships can I find in my family of origin?" "How do I distance from my colleagues at work?" "How do I distance from my friends?" Or, "How do I get them to distance from me?" An even better question may be: "What is the origin of the intensity that leads to the distance, or makes it necessary?"

As those intense reactions and reaction patterns are better understood, the need for distance becomes less and less pronounced. As with all the relationship patterns, just taking a look through the lens of family systems principles can lend clarity of thought and objectivity about one's own role in the process.

If distancing is seen as an attempt to work out the individuality/togetherness problem, is there a way to do it that would calm emotions rather than intensify them further? Mr. and Mrs. D found avoiding meaningful contact with each other was deadly, not only to their relationship, but to the individuality of each partner. When they began to experiment with making contact on a fairly regular basis, even if that contact was brief, they found they had more freedom to work on their individual life issues than they did when they avoided the relationship by a patterned distance.

If a relationship is stuck in feeling intensity, disguised outwardly by superficiality, silence, and avoidance, it is important to get in touch with the emotional intensity that underlies the distant stance. If one does not, to some degree, differentiate self from the togetherness that generates that intensity, one will usually try another relationship posture in the interest of doing something different. The solution for a relationship posture is not another posture, however, nor is it intense closeness. Rather, intense closeness is one of the stances of relationship fusion from which distance may ultimately develop. When people can get to calm, thoughtful definition of self that comes from thought-out principles, they are on their way out of a pattern.

When Mrs. D understood that, in her marriage, distance was partly a reaction to her own emotional intensity, she could see the importance of managing herself differently. As she dumped less feeling intensity into the relationship, she perceived less distance from her partner. Less distance from him was calming to her, so a different, more productive kind of relationship interaction developed.

Her changes did not have the solid emotional underpinnings she hoped for until she took a long hard look at the family she grew up in and worked to change her reactions there. During her childhood, her parents had a conflictual relationship. When fights would break out, she would cover her head with the bed covers or hide in a closet. In her teenage years, her parents divorced. After that, she and her three younger siblings saw little of their father. She developed a rich fantasy life about creating a different kind of family. How hard could it be to just get along? As an adult, with avoiding conflict as her only guiding principle, she found herself and her husband simply avoiding each other. Important issues were not defined.

She began to work on herself by making an effort to bring meaning, not only into her relationship with her husband, but also with her mother. She had only a superficial relationship with her mother as well, fearing the kind of conflict she witnessed between her mother and her siblings. Now, without blaming or trying to change anyone, she dared to ask questions about the family and her mother's role in it. Some questions were unwelcome: about her mother's parents' relationship, her mother's relationship with her father, and her father's family. This effort led, of course, straight towards conflict. Mrs. D anticipated it and was ready. She met her mother's reactions with calm, thoughtful responses, which became easier the more she understood about her mother's place in her own emotional system.

In time, she even made contact with her father, whom she had not seen for several years. As she came more into contact with him and his family, the other fifty percent of the problem in her original family became clearer. As she continued the hard work, over years, of getting into the emotional field of her extended family and becoming more the present and responsible self she wanted to be in it, her reactions in her own nuclear family were less intense, giving her more choice in them. She gained, over time, more ability to think her way through emotionally triggering events, avoiding her tendency to run or hide from real issues. She was, in short, more of a self.

Simple, calm, person-to-person contact is elusive for many people. Learning how to make meaningful human contact after a lifetime of distancing is no easy task. For people in a distant relationship, it is sometimes useful to make contact with a partner or other person for even a few minutes out of every day. Letting the other person know what is going on inside one's head is balanced by attending to the expressions of the other, verbal as well as non-verbal. Most distanced people will not tolerate more than short periods of meaningful contact in the beginning. However, over time, they often find that their emotional reactivity to exchanging real meaning, in openness, decreases.

What is making contact? It is hard to define, but people do know when they have or have not made contact. It is something that animals are very good at, judging by various reports from ethologists who talk of apes extending an open hand to one another, of grooming, or of sexual contact. Sometimes it seems that humans have lost the art. The range of possibilities for contact open to human beings is extremely large, ranging from conversations that can last hours to something as brief as a pull on a pigtail. However, just a small attempt to make contact with the other person on a regular basis can put a distant relationship back on track.

CUTOFF

The principal manifestation of the emotional cutoff is denial of the intensity of the unresolved emotional attachment to parents, acting and pretending to be more independent than one is, and emotional distance achieved either through internal mechanisms or physical distance.

Murray Bowen, 1974

Mrs. U had been on antidepressants for years. She consulted a psychiatrist to get a refill when her family physician refused to keep her on them any longer without psychiatric advice. When the psychiatrist asked her about her family relationships, she found that Mrs. U was very close to her grown son and his family and, in fact, could be said to be devoting most of her life's energy to that family, helping them in any way she could. She baby-sat, cooked, cleaned, and, in general, spent a great deal of time in their home. Her marriage was stable and calm, if a little distant. Most of her family of origin was deceased, although she had one sister living in a distant city whom she had not seen in years. She once told the story of how it had hurt long ago when the sister suddenly married and left town with no explanation, never contacting the family again.

That hurt apparently had stood in the way of Mrs. U's making contact with her sister for many years. She was definitely not motivated to get in touch with her at the beginning of therapy. The psychiatrist wondered if the depressive symptoms she was experiencing could possibly be related to the cutoff from members of her family of origin. Mrs. U became intrigued by the idea that her symptoms might improve if she made an effort to bridge the cutoff with her sister.

Mrs. U summoned up her courage and sent a friendship card and a brief note to her sister. In a few days she received a long, warm letter. Correspondence continued, followed by phone calls. Finally, they made plans for a reunion. After that Mrs. U noticed that her antidepressant medication was too strong; the dose had to be lowered repeatedly. Within a few weeks, she was off the medication. As she worked on mending the cutoff with her family of origin, her depression receded. Since many physicians had told her that she would probably always need antidepressants, Mrs. U was amazed and delighted when the need for them disappeared.

Cutoff is a distant posture carried to the extreme, a nonfunctioning relationship. Quite often the cutoff is so old that all the people involved have forgotten what originally triggered it. America has sometimes been called a nation of cutoffs, since it was settled largely by immigrants. Whatever the cultural contribution to it, cutoff is such a common pattern among American families that it is often hard to see. It may even be seen as a desirable state of affairs. It seems that the American way of growing up is to leave home and never return again, at least emotionally. When one leaves home, meaningful relationships with one's family of origin are often severed. Visits are limited to those of the "duty" or the "ritual" variety at holidays.

The stimulus that precipitates cutoff may be erroneously viewed as the reason for the cutoff. Stimuli may include problems over money. Sometimes people cut off from each other at the time of a family divorce, if sides are taken. Religious differences may stand out in an intensity of feelings finally managed by cutoff. These precipitating circumstances stand out as "the cause" in the minds of people who are cutoff from each other.

In fact, cutoff develops as an attempt to adapt to intense chronic and acute anxiety in the system. If we study the family system of one who is involved in cutoff relationships, we will usually find that there is more than just one instance of cutoff in the family. In fact, most often, many generations will have taken part in the same patterned response to intense feelings. It is only an end point in a long family emotional process.

It is more profitable to look at the process itself rather than the end point. Undifferentiation leads to fusion of selfs, which produces anxiety, which gets triggered around a given issue. Yet, because the intensity of feelings makes it impossible for anyone to think clearly, individuals respond with emotionally based action, the knee jerk family reaction pattern of cutoff. Undifferentiation has moved one more time, through one more generation.

Issues, such as money, divorce, or religion, may provide the battleground, but undifferentiation in the members of the family is the real problem. In a more mature group, these issues get handled in a way short of cutoff. Unfortunately, what the cutting off individuals don't understand is that there is a price to be paid for emotional cutoff. The price is a very dear one.

Cutoff can ameliorate emotional intensities or symptoms temporarily, but over time it will actually have the effect of increasing them. That is why, with the exception of a brief period of calm (or even euphoria) immediately following the cutoff, people involved in cut off relationships begin to experience an intensification of depression and anxiety. They find themselves unable to cope with life's problems—socially adrift, suffering from addictions, or getting embroiled in legal entanglements. Sometimes there is merely a general failure to succeed. The brief period of euphoria after the cutoff throws people off track; it is the deceptive part of the pattern that prevents an understanding of the link between the cutoff and the later increase of emotional symptoms.

Cutoff, linked with poor relationships, means that relationships in the workplace, friendships, and even romances will not be as smooth for people who are cut off from their families of origin as they will be for people who are in contact with their family of origin. Because the emotional systems of cut off people tend to be smaller, the relationships they do have are more intense. A pattern of cutoff is like a cancer that spreads into all areas of life (Fig. 7).

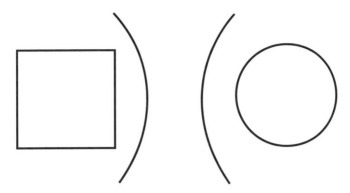

Figure 7. Cutoff

Consider the plot of a hypothetical generic opera. The tenor and the soprano meet. They are instantly attracted. They fall in love. They are full of fervent, passionate feelings that are lyricized and dramatized on the stage. But alas, almost as suddenly as their passion develops, another mood appears. Now the fervent, passionate love turns into fierce, fiery rancor. Invectives are hurled. The two separate. They go their singular ways into the world. As they wander the earth for years, they never cease to think of one another. They dream and fantasize about each other. "If only I could be back with him (her), my life would be wonderful!"

One day, by chance, they meet. They are ecstatic. They embrace. Their love is again lyricized, dramatized. In the next scene, however, they begin to wonder, "Where have you been all this time?" "Why didn't you find me sooner?" They begin to argue. Within minutes, the intense ecstasy turns to intense anxiety, anger, and pain. Quickly, we are given to understand how their emotional process led to cutoff in the first place.

When the emotional intensity that powered the attraction became negative, it acted like a repelling magnetic force. One wonders, does the powerful positive-feelings phase itself somehow induce the negative phase? If the tenor and the soprano had allowed their emotional intensity to develop more slowly, less lavishly, would their relationship have fared better?

Mrs. U, who knew very little about her extended family, began to explore the phenomenon of cutoff in it. She found cutoff so prevalent that there were entire branches of her family she did not know existed. The more she learned about emotional process in her family, the more she understood her own tendency to cut off. As she included more people in her family and in her life, there was less intensity in her marriage and within herself to deal with.

When cutoff occurs, what can be done to change it? As a first step, the pattern must be recognized. Often a cutoff person indulges in lesser forms of cutoff on a regular basis. Distancing maneuvers may be repeated many times in any given day. When people become familiar with their own patterns, they are in a position to recognize the anxiety that lies beneath the patterned behavior.

Working with that anxiety itself may be more productive than trying to change the distancing or cutoff pattern that is only the symptom of the anxiety. Since most of our anxieties are out of proportion to the circumstances that trigger them, they will often be calmed by thinking about them, getting the bigger picture. Techniques like exercise, biofeedback training or relaxation exercises, sports, recreational activities, or pleasurable pursuits can be extremely useful in regaining perspective. Any relationship may become overtaxed if the partners routinely bring their emotional reactions into it.

As with the other relationship patterns, it may be useful to ask: "What is my part in this cutoff?" Better yet, "What is my part in inducing the intensity of feeling that made the cutoff inevitable?" and "Is there anything I might do to bridge the cutoff?" "Is there a way I can work to lower my emotional intensity so cutoff will not be inevitable in the future?"

And of course, working to bridge cutoffs in one's family of origin carries the greatest rewards for the self. Cutoff can never be changed unless someone takes responsibility for him -or herself in the cutoff and begins to move responsibly in the relationship.

OVERFUNCTIONING/UNDERFUNCTIONING

RECIPROCITY

> This is the result when a significant amount of undifferentiation is absorbed in the adaptive posture of one spouse. The pseudo self of the adaptive one merges into the pseudo self of the dominant one, who assumes more and more responsibility for the twosome.
>
> **Murray Bowen, 1976**

Mr. and Mrs. R never went on vacation. They couldn't. Mrs. R's physical and emotional health were too unpredictable. Most of the time she didn't feel like doing anything except staying home. She felt miserable all the time, but doctors couldn't find the source of her symptoms. When she wasn't physically ill, she was depressed. She and Mr. R would sometimes go to see their grown children, but she never enjoyed the trips and was always glad to go home again.

Mrs. R worried a great deal about what she would do if her husband ever left her. She considered that a real possibility since she knew she must be a very difficult person to be around. She berated herself continually: "I know what I should do. Everyone tells me I should get involved in life, in activities, or a job. I should exercise. I should diet and lose all this weight. I just don't do any of it. I can't. I'm not motivated. Doctor, please help me. Please tell me what to do!"

Mr. R was successful. He could be away from his work whenever necessary, which was fortunate since Mrs. R needed him at home a great deal of the time. When he looked back over their lives together, he wondered what had gone wrong. During the earlier years, when he had been building a business and she was raising their two children, Mrs. R had done quite well. She had small bouts of depression now and then, but they were easily cleared by prescriptions that her family doctor gave her. Now that they had more time and money, they were able to do and have practically anything they wanted, but Mrs. R was too ill to enjoy life. Mr. R had tried everything he could think of to help her.

He gave advice: "What you need are some interests. Look at me. I'm on the board of several organizations. I enjoy many friends, many activities. I enjoy my career greatly, and I love to travel. We could be traveling more now. There are so many places I'd like to go and people I'd like to see. I want us to do these things together."

He took most of the responsibility for the household and for the relationship. He cooked almost all their meals when they didn't eat out. He did the laundry on the weekends and saw to it they had competent household help. The more he did for her, the sicker she seemed to be. She never took any of his suggestions. That was the part that was hardest to understand. The active approach to life and helping other people had worked so well for him. He knew that if she would try this, it would work for her, too. But she seemed unwilling to do anything for herself—or was she really too sick to try?

Mrs. R, for her part, agreed with everything her husband said. Yet she could not bring herself to attempt any of his suggestions. When she did, to please him, she was more miserable than usual. She spent a lot of time worrying about what would become of her if anything happened to him. She knew she was not the partner to her husband that she wanted to be. What if he should leave her? When he became impatient with her and all of her complaints, she really worried about that possibility. And yet, year after weary year, nothing ever seemed to change.

Mr. and Mrs. R had created a relationship of overfunctioning/underfunctioning reciprocity, where one person of the pair does quite well in life, standing in happy contrast to the despair and dysfunction of the other. One is the teller, the other the listener; one the preacher, one the congregation. Both partners usually agree that one of them is doing well, and that "the problem" rests solely in the dysfunctional one.

This way of handling relationship fusion, or exchange of self in a relationship, is often termed the "dysfunctional spouse" posture because of the frequency with which the submissive or adaptive spouse becomes symptomatic. The partners in an overfunctioning/ underfunctioning relationship have varying degrees of understanding as to how the relationship itself brings about the dependency and illness of the underfunctioning spouse. One of the two may see that the relationship contributes to the illness but has no idea how to break the long-standing pattern. While the overfunctioner in this example is male, the roles are just as often the reverse.

Overfunctioning/underfunctioning reciprocity can be diagrammed as follows:

Figure 8. Overfunctioning/underfunctioning reciprocity.

If overfunctioning is present, one might see:
- advice-giving
- doing things for others that they could do for themselves
- worrying about other people
- feeling responsible for others, knowing what is best for them
- talking more than listening
- having goals for others that they don't have for themselves
- experiencing periodic, sudden "burnouts"

In an underfunctioning state, one might see:
- asking for advice when what is needed is to think things out independently
- getting others to help when help really is not needed

- acting irresponsibly
- listening more than talking
- floating without goals much of the time
- setting goals but not following through with them
- becoming mentally or physically ill frequently
- tending to become addicted to substances

Both partners often think of the overfunctioning partner as healthier, more independent, and more complete than the underfunctioning partner. Actually this is not the case. The overfunctioner is just as caught in this relationship process as the underfunctioner. Often overfunctioners, though they may lead productive lives much of the time, may themselves be subject to sudden physical illness or "burnout" because of the stress involved in taking responsibility for two people.

Overfunctioning/underfunctioning may or may not be a total way of life for any individual. In all the relationship postures, there are degrees of expression, and there are patterns within patterns. The tyrannical boss at work may be underfunctioning in his relationship at home. Or a couple may be seen to take turns in the two positions, one overfunctioning for a while, or on some issues, then underfunctioning while the other overfunctions at other times or on other issues.

Therapists joke "Every overfunctioner deserves his under-functioner." Family systems theory tells us that each partner in a relationship is exactly as differentiated or emotionally mature as the other; otherwise the two wouldn't attract. This often comes as quite a shock to the overfunctioner who thinks he or she is the healthy, more adequate, or more talented member of the pair.

The fact of the matter is, however, that the success of the overfunctioner takes place in the context of a relationship barter that is an effort to make a self out of two. This is to the advantage of the overfunctioner. He or she takes on the functional self of the other, who loses self into the relationship.

When the partners in this relationship are ready for equality of functioning, they can find ways to work toward it. If the overfunctioner will stop overfunctioning (that is, take responsibility for the self, and only for the self, communicate for the self and only for the self), often the underfunctioner will begin to stop underfunctioning to a reciprocal degree. In the same way, the underfunctioning partner can take the initiative for changing the relationship by changing the part that he or she contributes. This partner can begin to take responsibility for his or her self and for his or her decisions. When each can take responsibility for self in the relationship there is a concomitant responsibility, that of communicating or defining self to the other.

In any case, when either partner takes the initiative for being responsible for self and only self and communicates that to the other, an initial flurry of protest can be expected from the other. Although it may become rather intense, this reaction will be brief if the initiating partner stays on course and steadily continues to take responsibility for changing her or his own contribution to the problem. Following that phase, the partnership can be expected to regroup at a higher level of functioning.

The decision to initiate change brought fear and trembling for Mr. R since most of his thinking in recent memory had been focused on his wife's problems. Once he decided to make a move for himself, with consequences to himself paramount in his mind, he began literally to fear divorce or death. When he understood that his decision would entail neither, he became free to move differently.

Mr. R's first action was a nonaction: He thought. He recalled family systems principles. Thinking about individuality and togetherness forces, he saw that he and Mrs. R were locked in a togetherness pattern that was consuming them both. He convinced himself that, for his part, he needed to find a way to become more of an individual—an individual defined more in terms of himself rather than the needs of others.

Watching for process allowed him to see his part in the problem. He quickly saw that he almost always put consideration of other people ahead of consideration of himself, and he often exhausted himself in order to take care of them. Somehow, though, serving other people's needs made Mr. R feel good, and it was probably a factor in his impressive success in the world.

Process watching also enabled Mr. R to become familiar with behaviors in other people that triggered his overfunctioning. If someone asked him for advice, he was all too ready to give it. If a friend asked for help, he was there whether or not it was in his own or his friend's best interest.

Thinking systems, Mr. R saw both his and his wife's positions clearly. He began to understand how his overfunctioning not only permitted but actually facilitated his wife's illness. Thinking about the family system he grew up in, he saw how, from an early age, he had been an overfunctioner. Early on, he had taken responsibility for the younger children in his family. His mother, a single parent, had been subject to bouts of withdrawal into alcoholism and was often not available to be a parent. The role of virtual parent to his five younger siblings had continued into his adulthood. His siblings often called him for advice or financial support. They looked to him to organize the family around special occasions. His overfunctioning role was also obvious at work, where he often took on other people's problems as though they were his own.

In order for Mr. R to begin the project of differentiating a self, he had to think about how he could be responsible for himself and for himself only. For the first time in his life, he had to find a way to put himself first while he continued to be present and accounted for in his important systems—with his wife, his grown children and their families, his employees, and the people he grew up with.

Mr. R started to define himself to his wife—what he was and was not willing and able to do. He realized, for example, that by automatically having answers for his wife, he implied she did not have nor could she get them for herself. He made it his goal to refrain from doing things or finding answers for others that they could do or find for themselves. Shortly thereafter, as he let go of the borrowed self he'd had available to him for years and began to operate only from his own self, he experienced mood changes. When other people reacted to his different stance, he found the temptation to snap back into old patterns strong. But he realized that an effort to increase his own resources—his own amount of basic self—was a better solution, and he stayed on course.

Mrs. R learned her husband would not always be available in the ways he formerly had been. This raised her anxiety. Temporarily she became sicker. She became angry. She threatened Mr. R, but he stayed on course. Managing the illness more on her own, however, increased her confidence in her coping ability. She allowed herself to do more on her own—she became more of a self.

Eventually she became quite grateful for Mr. R's moves for self and told him so. At this point, each was functioning at a higher level, and there was more equality in the relationship. As Mrs. R gained more emotional independence, her health slowly improved.

When people who are ready to make changes are asked who they feel equal to in their systems, the answer is often "no one." People mired in this stance will sometimes feel above or below everyone in their extended families and work places. Teaching oneself to feel equal in relationships can be a major task.

Several combined circumstances in their growing up triangles may have helped to entrench people in the overfunctioning/ underfunctioning pattern. Sometimes, overfunctioners are older children in their families of origin, and underfunctioners are younger children. If they were not actually the oldest or the youngest, they may have been the oldest or the youngest in subgroupings of the siblings within their families, so they had to take more or less responsible positions *vis-a-vis* their siblings. They may simply have had a position of responsibility and overfunctioning thrust upon them. Quite frequently, the partners had parents with similar marital patterns of overfunctioning or underfunctioning. Sometimes they had parents who, caught in their own family patterns, relied on them as though they were parents instead of children. And sometimes the pattern was not experienced at all in early years. It may be simply the way undifferentiation is working itself out in this generation.

In any case, placing blame is inappropriate. A systems thinker will immediately realize that anyone's parents also had parents of their own who were caught in their own patterns, and so on, back through the generations. In Mr. R's case, his underfunctioning mother had been the focus of her hovering mother who had taken care of her beyond an appropriate age. She thus remained dependent. As an adult, Mr. R's mother found a way to continue her emotionally dependent, underfunctioning pattern through one of her children.

To begin the work of changing a relationship of overfunctioning/underfunctioning reciprocity, one must not ask, "How can I change this troublesome partner of mine?" Instead the question is, "What is my contribution to this relationship pattern?" The task becomes one of teaching oneself to be responsible for self and only for self. That means, for the overfunctioner, thinking, planning, and being concerned more of the time with self and management of self than with management of the other. Also, it rules out taking responsibility for doing for someone else anything they can easily do for self. Likewise, the underfunctioner will not ask for help when it is really not needed. The burden of responsibility for one's happiness will not be placed on the other; rather, responsibility for feeling good or bad, as well as for one's thoughts and behavior, rests solely with the self. There will be, of course, some reactive turmoil whenever one sets out to change one's part of any of the relationship patterns. In most cases, however, the turmoil is short-lived. If solid work on the self is pursued, the relationship eventually finds higher ground as each finds a little more of the emotional maturity that comes with a greater level of differentiation of self.

TRIANGLES

The concept of triangles provides a theoretical framework for understanding the microscopic functioning of all emotional systems. . . . . A two-person emotional system is unstable in that it forms itself into a three-person system or triangle under stress.

Murray Bowen, 1972

It wasn't that Mr. and Mrs. T were not caring parents. On the contrary, they were committed students of the subject of child-rearing. In preparation for the birth of their first child, Mrs. T read many books on child care covering both physical and emotional issues. The couple attended several classes on parenting. By any standards, they would be considered nurturing parents. Yet, Mrs. T and, to a lesser degree, Mr. T, found themselves worrying a great deal about their children. Both considered being parents one of the most important job of an adult's life, and both felt ill-prepared for the task.

Mrs. T's mother had been a worrier, too, and had had some major bouts with depression while Mrs. T was growing up. So one of Mrs. T's major concerns was how not to be worried or depressed, as her mother had been.

Mr. T, in the early years of their marriage, had had a drinking problem. When his wife threatened to leave him if he didn't stop drinking, he attended Alcoholics Anonymous and quit drinking.

Now their conversations mostly centered around their first child, eight-year-old Melissa, and her problems. She did not do well in school, even though both of her parents were bright and well educated. She had no friends. She had a rather unhappy look on her face most of the time. Mr. and Mrs. T became completely preoccupied with how to help Melissa achieve in school, make friends, and feel better. Family outings were always for the whole family, including both Melissa and six-year-old Bryan. In fact, the children were included in everything. The couple took no vacations without the children. Of course, the more difficulty Melissa experienced, the more her parents worried. Most of their conversations with her were anxious ones.

In their first session with a consultant, Mr. and Mrs. T both denied there were any problems in their relationship. Everything between the two of them was fine. Of course, there had been that brief period of Mr. T's drinking in the beginning, but both people tended to minimize that. At this time, they considered the drinking chapter of their relationship closed. They were, however, capable of spending many hours describing their worries and concerns about their daughter in great detail.

The consultant wondered about the relationship between the worrying of the parents and the underfunctioning of the child. As Mrs. T recalled her own emotional reactions to her mother's worries, these parents were gradually able to lessen their focus on Melissa. As they focused more on their own lives and less on the daughter, Melissa's response was positive. In time, her friendships, school achievement, and mood were all on course.

As soon as Melissa began to do better, however, her parents came into their sessions with rather graphic details of their own relationship distress. Mr. T found a thousand and one ways to distance from Mrs. T, which put her in hot, anxious pursuit of him. The more he distanced, the more she pursued. With the focus on their child diminished, the two were at a point where they were able to work on their relationship.

A two-person relationship is a delicate thing, prone to collapse in several different ways. Triangling—bringing into focus a third party, rather than solving the relationship problem of the original twosome—is only one of the many ways primary two-person relationship problems can be avoided. The T's set up what therapists often refer to as a "child-focused family." Rather than dealing with their own undifferentiation, they focused on their daughter. Once the "child focus" was modified, however, the distance in the marriage became evident.

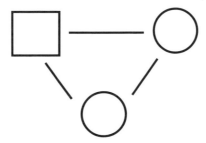

Figure 9. Triangling.

Some common manifestations of triangling include:

- talking against the boss, the minister, or the teacher to people other than the boss, the minister, or the teacher
- gossiping or talking about someone who is not present
- having an affair
- taking a morbid interest in other people's problems
- thinking more about a child or anyone else than about one's marriage or oneself.

If partners in a triangled relationship want to be on a more direct, one-to-one basis, they need first to see the triangle and how it enables the primary partners to avoid each other. When the partners of a triangled relationship take a look at their old patterns, they often find they were themselves the over-focus of one or both parents. Many learn that their parents frequently triangled as a means of avoiding their own relationship difficulties.

When Mrs. T began to think about the principles of Bowen family systems theory, she found that when Melissa was born, her own individuality had been completely submerged into togetherness with the baby, just as her own mother's had been. Since she had become a mother, she had taken no time to pursue her own goals. Individuality was sadly lacking in her life. Recognizing this, she was in a position to think about her life objectives. Out of this examination she gained a clearer definition of where she wanted to go; she launched an exploration of career possibilities and eventually enrolled in a training program.

Mrs. T also looked at her family system. In her extended family, she could see many distanced relationships, as well as several families with an intense child focus. She began to contact relatives from whom she had been cut off for years. That work facilitated her moving differently in her marriage. Just beginning to think about the problem got her focus off Melissa, which provided relief to everyone in the family.

Once she could see the problem, Mrs. T looked at the process to see how distance and triangling worked in both her nuclear and extended families. As she gained more understanding about that process, she learned how they worked in her own emotional patterns. She looked at emotional reactivity—how it traveled and became patterned through the triangles in her family—in as much detail as possible.

Then she studied her own emotional process. She looked at what triggered her to distance and what triggered her to triangle. She examined the emotional intensity needed to set off her patterned behaviors. She could see how, and when, the distancing tendency ended up in triangling. She began to think of ways to relate to her husband that kept the focus on managing her emotional self better.

Working on herself in the context of her family of origin was an important component of her effort to change her old patterns. Her initial efforts were tentative at first and stressful. Still, she sought time with her father, mother, and siblings in her efforts to modify her emotional reactivity among those various triangles.

Mrs. T's older sister had received even more parental focus than Mrs. T had. While growing up, this situation had often triggered anger, frustration, and jealousy in Mrs. T. As she found more effective ways to relate to the people in the triangle that existed between her mother, her sister, and herself, all her old feelings came back. Her efforts to keep her feelings calm while staying in relationship to that triangle—not distancing from it and not forming another triangle—were monumental. Logic told her she was now an adult and had no reason to be in the grip of strong emotion when her mother focused more on her sister than on herself. But the feelings were there, nonetheless. In time, her work began to pay off, and she was able to be less emotionally intense in the triangle, while staying in open communication with both her mother and her sister. As a result of this effort, she learned a great deal about doing her part of all her relationships better.

It is automatic that when anxiety rises between two people, they turn to a third and include that person in the situation in some way. This triangular arrangement seems to be more stable. It seems to continue longer and to contain the anxiety better than can the twosome. Triangles are ubiquitous and automatic in emotional systems. They are considered, in Bowen family systems theory, to be the molecule, or basic building block of any system of people—be it the family, an organization, or society itself. The goal is not how to get out of them, however, but rather how to manage oneself in and through them.

Triangles connect all family members and are almost innumerable in any good-sized family (Fig. 10). Triangles connect to each other through a series of interlocks to the members of the extended families. Through further interlocking triangles with societal organizations and relationships, family connects with family and organization with organization.

When anxiety is more intense in the family or in society, triangles are more apparent. Conversely, when the system under observation is more calm, triangles are less noticeable. The more undifferentiated the emotional system is, the more intense the triangling or flow of anxiety through triangles.

The most common and important triangle that people find when they begin to examine their patterns is the one that was formed between themselves and their two parents or caregivers at birth. However, there are multiple triangles in any family or organization of more than three people.

Figure 10.

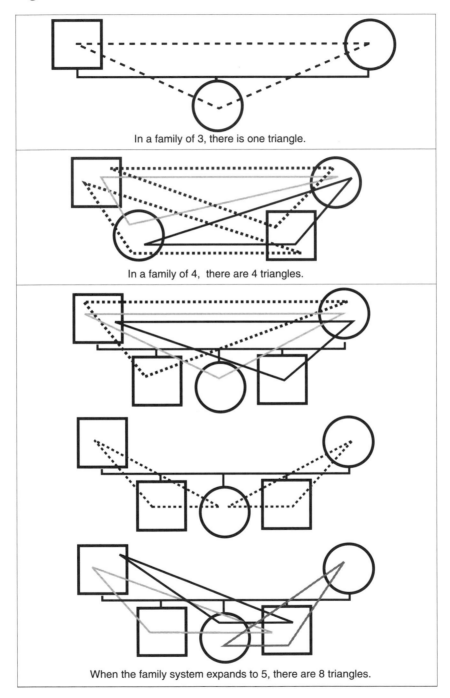

In a family of 3, there is one triangle.

In a family of 4, there are 4 triangles.

When the family system expands to 5, there are 8 triangles.

It takes considerable mental effort to manage oneself in a triangle. Seeing the other two in it as together and accepting the situation calmly can be a challenge. When one can calmly link the other two together in thought and even in conversation, working for emotional neutrality toward each, one has begun to learn something about managing oneself in the triangles of an emotional system.

It is important to become aware of all the forms that triangles take. In everyday life, they turn up in innocent activities, such as asking a third person to settle a disagreement between two others. In churches, workplaces, or social groups, triangles are ever-present, but they are more apparent and intense when anxiety is running higher.

Once triangling is identified, it becomes possible to think about managing oneself in it. A primary question is, "What is my contribution to this pattern?" Or "How am I triangling?" followed by "How do I go about changing my part of the triangle?" That is, "What do I have to do to get emotionally more neutral and still communicate with both other parts of the triangle?"

What are the basic principles of managing the self in a triangle? First, staying in calm, open communication with the other parts of a triangle is useful, managing one's emotions so as not to take on the anxiety of the other two. The preferable position in an intense triangle is often the outside one.

The B's spent endless hours in tense concern over the rebellious behavior of their son Jack. Once Mr. B had decided it was not in anyone's best interest to continue to worry about Jack's actions, his problem was how to get emotionally neutral in the triangle, without distancing from either person. He made it his policy from then on to find ways of being in calm contact with both his wife and Jack. Mr. B occasionally found ways to let Jack know, without preaching or telling him what to do, more about what guiding principles Mr. B would choose if he were faced with Jack's situations. That is, he talked with his son out of his own principles. At the same time, he did not hesitate to impose limits and remind Jack of the consequences when his behavior was inappropriate or inconvenient to the rest of the family.

As soon as Mr. B got a little more neutral, the intense "child-focused" triangle became an intense dyad between Mrs. B and Jack. Mr. B then made a new effort, working toward emotional calm in himself whenever intensities arose between his wife and son. Where once his wife's upsets about Jack would cause Mr. B a great deal of anxiety, he now began to work on merely observing their interactions with as little emotional reactivity as possible.

An acceptance of the other two as together in an emotional intensity enabled him to get some inner calm. He took pains not to distance from the others, however. While working to reduce his own intensities, he continued to talk and listen to both, often putting the two of them together in his conversation with one or the other. No matter how anxious Mrs. B became over Jack's behavior, Mr. B calmly listened, responded with his calmer view of things, and always included his opinion that Jack had everything he needed to grow into a mature, responsible adult. He expressed confidence that their son would no doubt accomplish that task. He also expressed confidence that Jack and his mother could work out the differences between them, but he never offered suggestions or advice as to how they were to do this.

Mr. B allowed himself no more sleepless nights. He made it his business to concentrate on his own life problems more than on anyone else's. Gradually, Mrs. B saw the value of this approach. As she began to work more on controlling her own anxiety over their son, she was able to think about her own life course more calmly, something she had long postponed. She also started learning to communicate with her son, instead of continually worrying about him. Soon Jack began to emulate his parents in taking a thoughtful interest in his own life direction, a path more independent of automatic rebellion.

It is simplistic to advocate that if you stop worrying about your children, they'll automatically have no problems. To be alive is to have problems. But it is certain that, if children don't have their parents' concern about them added to their ordinary difficulties, they will do better. Worrying about a child does not solve the lack of differentiation of self that leads to it.

It is interesting in a child-focused or romantic triangle to speculate on what the marital pattern would be if there were no triangle. When the anxiety in the triangle becomes less intense, the pattern usually shows itself promptly.

Triangles are neither good nor bad. They just are, everywhere. As long as there is any undifferentiation left in the emotional system there will be triangles. For that reason, there is no possibility of going on to a higher level of differentiation without learning how to manage oneself emotionally in and through triangles. As one goes to a higher level of differentiation, the ability to recognize and manage oneself emotionally in triangles improves. But this ability will always remain relative.

REPETITIONS

Another idea important to understanding how humans behave in relationships is the tendency to repeat old patterns.

Sigmund Freud was the first to observe the existence and significance of the phenomenon he called "transference." He believed that certain cliches (they could be ideas, behaviors, attitudes, or feelings) got established early in life and subsequently resided in what he thought of as the unconscious mind. He believed that in later life these cliches became attached to other cliches with an inappropriate emotional strength.

On this point, the relationship between Freudian and Bowen theory is similar to that between Einsteinian and Newtonian physics. Einsteinian theory, rather than completely invalidating Newtonian theory, incorporated it into a larger and more general theoretical structure. Bowen theory, taking as it does a larger look, is more extensive and explains more of the facts than does Freudian theory. However, Bowen theory does not completely invalidate Freudian theory. Systems thinkers use a broader frame of reference, keeping in mind more variables, and thus the way they approach everything is changed.

Bowen agreed that the phenomenon Freud called transference is in nature, but he thought about it much differently. In Bowen theory, there is no unconscious, nor "psychic energy," both of which were necessary to explain the transference phenomenon from Freud's standpoint. A way of understanding the phenomenon of tranference from the new point of view became necessary.

One way to think about it is seeing these repeating reactions and behaviors as patterns of emotions and functioning that are impressed on the emotional system of an individual early in life. This occurs through repetition of these patterns in early triangles of the individual's family of origin. They are experienced and acted out throughout life—unless and until the individual acquires replacement patterns of reaction or moves to a level of differentiation that affords more choice of response.

MacLean sees the tendency toward repetition as originating in the reptilian brain. Lorenz studied the imprinting phenomenon that occurs in specific windows of time in which animals are especially vulnerable. For example, when he studied the imprinting phenomenon in geese, he found that if a human instead of a mother goose were first presented to the hatchlings in that crucial time period, the goslings would follow the human instead of their mother. Once imprinted, the response continued indefinitely.

This phenomenon is certainly seen in the human. But because the new theory sees everything so differently, renaming it may make sense. The designation "reactive repetition" or simply "repetition" may suffice. Seen from the new perspective, repetitions are *patterned behavior or feeling states formed in early relationship triangles in the family of origin*. The behavior patterns are dictated by patterns imprinted in early life. Since they are relationship-determined, they take the form of the well-known relationship patterns of conflict, distance, cutoff, overfunctioning/underfunctioning reciprocity, or triangles.

In a well-differentiated person, fewer repetitions occur. Those that do are less intense and are better understood by the person as being rooted in the original relationship system. Better definition between thinking and emotional inner guidance systems enables one to tell the difference between reality and patterned functioning originating from within. Thus for the well-differentiated person, fewer emotional reactions from old patterns can be triggered by stimuli from other people.

Clearly, to the degree one is carrying around circuits in the brain and body physiology that are grounded in past relationships, one is not free to respond to present relationships with flexibility. Relationships are complicated by past relationship patterns. The more complicated and intense the relationships of the past, the more complicated the relationships of the present.

What can be done to change these repetitions when they are inappropriate and unwanted? The old theory advocated changing them in the context of the relationship with a therapist (analyzing the transference). The only problem was that often, though understanding of the reactions became fairly complete, the reactions did not go away. Working in the new paradigm, therapists are finding a different situation. If one can make emotional contact with the family of origin (where, of course, the repetition originated) and change the reaction in that context, over time, it will remain fundamentally changed. This is a more difficult assignment, but clinical experience with both ways of managing emotional reactivity suggests it is far more effective.

FAMILY CONSTELLATION
AND SIBLING POSITIONS

Social relationships are more enduring and successful the more they resemble the earlier and earliest (intrafamilial) social relationships of the persons involved.

Walter Toman, 1961

Dr. Walter Toman's work, *Family Constellation,* based on the study of 3,000 people, represents a major scientific advance, putting in place more pieces of the relationship puzzle. His studies led him to conclusions about how personality and relationship profiles were related to sibling position. These findings were eagerly assimilated by Bowen as he was formulating theory.

Going far towards explaining the "chemistry" of relationships, Toman's work moved the understanding of personality and relationships light years ahead. Even the mysteries of why people were attracted to each other yielded to his probing questions. So did the problem of preferences as well as some of the factors that go into forming enduring romantic, business, and friendly relationships. It may be that these characteristics, since they are automatic and rooted in the relationship system, are a particular form of repetition reactions.

Sibling position, Dr. Toman found, explained why some relationships require less and some more effort. His research also showed that sibling position has a great deal to do with how two people in a relationship behave toward each other. Theorists in human behavior have long believed that much of personality is formed early in the years spent in the family of origin, but it has been less clear as to what the important factors of the early years are. Dr. Toman's work identified the very order of a person's birth, as well as the mix of genders in that configuration, all other things being equal, as major determinants of personality characteristics.

In order to understand relationships and what part one may be playing in them, it is useful to understand something about how one's family constellation may have influenced one's personality formation at a very basic level. Toman's work also aids in the understanding and accepting of the others in the relationship system.

In Toman's Sibling Position Data (Appendix III), there are distinct "role portraits" of individuals based on sibling position, condensed from Toman's writing. Following that are descriptions of typical relationships into which the different sibling positions combine.

These portraits are to be understood merely as starting points in the important work of developing more self—not at all as end points or as unchangeable.

Based on sibling position alone, setting differentiation aside, some relationship patterns seem to come up more frequently than would be expected by chance alone. For example, a partnership of oldest siblings, when it gets stuck, often tends toward conflict. An oldest paired with a youngest, if they get into a pattern, may go toward an overfunctioning/underfunctioning reciprocity, with the oldest in the overfunctioning position and the youngest in the underfunctioning. A pair of youngests can sometimes flounder for lack of decision-making capability, each waiting for the other to take the lead, or perhaps taking turns telling each other what to do.

Sibling positions can be seen as deterministic. However, Toman believes people can profitably work to lessen their influence. And, given the human capacity for repetition, understanding what part that position played in the development of personality becomes a first and necessary part of learning how to surpass the limiting aspects of it. Pushing against those limiting aspects will often tend to automatically heighten the favors bestowed by sibling position in both individual and interpersonal functioning.

People of high levels of differentiation can form successful liaisons and partnerships with people in any of the sibling positions. In other words, at higher levels, sibling position becomes less and less relevant to forming and maintaining successful relationships.

Every sibling position carries with it certain benefits. Each also has its limiting aspects. The goal is to preserve the natural strengths conferred upon one by sibling position, while finding a way to go beyond its restrictions. In order to do that, it is necessary to understand what the sibling position is and all the various ways one is still operating in it. This will necessitate getting outside of oneself and observing one's behavior closely for automatic responses that were developed in early years but may now be inappropriate. Small, day-to-day behaviors may be as revealing as any. At the same time, it is helpful to understand one's parents' sibling position, since each parent is an important imprint upon every individual.

For example, when Mr. S saw his life-long problem of excessive dependence on other people (that is, expecting everyone to take care of him) stemmed from his sibling position as a youngest, he began to rework his relationships with his brothers and sisters. Instead of expecting them to do things for him and otherwise take responsibility in the relationships, he began to take more responsibility for his relationships with them. For example, he began to initiate contact with each of them more often. He then worked on seeing himself as an equal with each of them. After that, he worked toward feeling equal in their presence. This was a gradual process that actually took several years to accomplish, but as his work progressed, he noticed his wife's complaints about him diminishing.

Also, it is possible to experiment with behaving differently. How would it look and feel to do even small behaviors that are derived from one's sibling position differently? Rehearsing them in the head before trying them out in the real world can be useful. For example, Dr. M became aware that her frequent confrontations with her oldest son had everything to do with the fact she and her son were both oldest children. As such, both liked to assert rather than listen, both liked to tell people what to do, and both sought to have the last word in conversations. Something about this realization helped her to make a shift in relating to him. If she continued in her bold, frontal "oldest" style with him, she began to understand, he would turn out either completely compliant or angry and rebellious. She needed to find a way to allow and encourage his being a self in the relationship while she continued to be a self (not putting herself into the adaptive, shut-down or underfunctioning position). Managing herself differently than she ever had, she was able to listen more to what he had to say. She acknowledged his assertions, accepted the "oldest" responsible side of him, yielded more responsibility over to him, and became a different type of parent to him than she had before.

Of inestimable value to her in this effort was the work she did in her family of origin. She rethought her relationships with her siblings; as she began to see her siblings more as equals and less as "little" brothers and sisters, those relationships became friendships. Instead of always telling or advising them, she sometimes asked their opinions. More of the time she found a way to simply be there with them. Her relationship with her son lost its angry, confrontational mode and he blossomed into a leader. Mother and son began to gain genuine respect for one another.

With practice in relating to one's actual sibling(s) differently, with goals in mind, one sees progress. First attempts at changing any behavior are always awkward. As time goes by, however, change will occur. Interestingly, the gains are seen best in retrospect. Consulting with a systems-trained professional can be useful in nudging one out of accustomed positions and patterns.

Sibling position, one type of patterned functioning, thus illustrates the potency of early patterns in adult life, both within the individual and also in relationship systems. Knowledge of it makes it possible to plot a course toward transcending those limitations acquired early on.

WHEN RELATIONSHIPS
GO OFF COURSE

Emotional responsiveness can profoundly affect the course of a relationship.

Murray Bowen 1971

In *Annie Hall,* Woody Allen says to Annie: "A relationship is like a shark. It has to constantly move forward or it dies. I think what we got on our hands is a dead shark."

What has gone wrong in relationships that over time become frozen into a pattern? And why don't patterns provide relief from anxiety, since, as we have seen, that is their purpose?

Actually, relationship patterns do provide a certain amount of relief from relationship anxiety. At least they divert attention from the real problem. Partners may often be traveling well-rutted roads in their relationship patterns. They do not perceive the relationship anxiety that is there. Instead they see their child, the other woman or man, or various conflicted issues as "the problem." Apparently, it is easier for the human to focus on another triangled person or on peripheral issues than to see the relationship problems that exist behind those symptoms.

The real problem is, to some degree, that the partners in a difficult relations are "no-selfs." Too much of each self has been absorbed into the relationship. As the clinical examples have illustrated, the selfs have become fused, emotionally speaking, into a conglomerate that is only an imitation of a real self. In this predicament, the partners think, feel, and plan more around the other person than around self.

People stuck in relationship patterns are often quite aware of how they give up self. For example, if they are asked whether they spend more time thinking about self or about the other, they will readily admit they spend more time thinking about the other. A person who is underfunctioning knows how much he or she adapts in the relationship and can readily tell how. People in triangling patterns are often quite aware of how the loss of self in their primary relationships leads them to want to find better relationships or focus on someone else, other than the primary relationship. Conflicted partners are acutely aware of their other-orientation.

When so much life energy is taken up with a relationship, very little is left over to pursue a life direction; there is a definite sense of being off-course.

Possibly part of what makes a new relationship exciting is the fact that, at least as far as that relationship goes, both parties still have some self intact. They have not yet taken part in the borrowing and lending that leads to relationship anxiety and patterns. Once self has become lost or gained in a relationship, the problem becomes how to get it back. Not an easy proposition, but one that has been accomplished by some people to some degree, over time.

In finding a way to think about the problem, one takes a large leap toward solving it. If one can mentally step away from the relationship itself and look at it as objectively as possible, patterned postures will usually be evident. The borrowing and lending of self through the medium of the relationship's pattern becomes almost immediately apparent. At the point of this awareness, the work becomes most difficult. The goal of taking back all blame and discontinuing all relationship positioning and posturing promotes and coincides with taking unilateral responsibility for developing more basic self.

What one can learn about oneself, one's beliefs, preferences, the way one's emotional reactivity gets triggered and is managed—all become valuable first steps toward differentiation of more self. Knowledge of the family system one grew up in makes it possible to take differentiating steps from it, while staying in relationship with it.

If one person in a relationship works on getting self back out of a relationship fusion, the other will automatically protest the change in various ways at the beginning of this process. However, if the working person stays on course with his or her project of building more basic self, while getting functional self out of the relationship, in time the other will adjust and often will join the first partner in the long-term project of differentiation of self. When that happens, the relationship is perceived by both as functioning better.

As the people in a relationship become more and more differentiated, they will have fewer relationship problems. Because of the greater emotional maturity of the two partners, relationship issues, as well as people peripheral to the relationship, are kept in perspective. Communication improves. The relationship is not burdened with issues and emotions that it cannot bear.

The trading of self that occurs in patterned relationships is a function of undifferentiation. Thus, if each person will be true to the task of working on his or her own problem of differentiating a self, the relationship will improve in time. Unfortunately, many initial attempts are abortive because the partners unwittingly only experiment with a different relationship pattern and do not make a true change in level of differentiation of self.

Many people gain a great deal of personal experience with the various patterns in this way. Partners may sometimes try to fool themselves into thinking they have worked on differentiation of a self or they have equality in their relationship, by trading positions with their partners within the pattern. Thus, overfunctioners and underfunctioners may trade places many times during the course of the day, sensing on a feeling level that this has something to do with equality or emotional maturity. Or partners locked in the heat of conflict for years may tire of that and retreat into distance, believing they have made some fundamental change. However, this kind of change will not make for a better-functioning relationship. For that to occur, each self must be taken back out of the relationship to the extent possible and clearly defined, first to the self and then communicated to the other on an ongoing basis.

All of this, for most people, will be a lifelong project having more to do with process than with end point. It is the kind of work that catalyzes the living of a life guided by inner direction and motivation. Color and stimulation are not lacking along the way if one takes the challenge of differentiation of self seriously.

II

Portrait of an Extraordinary Relationship

Portrait of an Extraordinary Relationship

> All things being equal, the life course of people is determined by the amount of unresolved emotional attachment, the amount of anxiety that comes from it, and the way they deal with this anxiety.
>
> **Murray Bowen, 1974**

Presently, there is very little in the general culture to prepare people to move toward extraordinary relationships. Rather, what is usually described on television, in movies, or in novels is an early and intense emotional experience where people base their initial involvement on feelings and then guide themselves through the relationship by interpreting these feelings to each other. The intensity normally seen in these cultural representations leads often enough toward a fiery emotional cutoff. Thus, instead of moving people toward excellence in relationships, cultural images of "normal" mitigate against it.

Stable, satisfying relationships do exist. The best relationships seem to enhance rather than hinder the individuality of both people. Yet, relationships usually function to fulfill the togetherness pull that emanates from undifferentiation. If relationships are used in an attempt to complete the self, not only will the self remain incomplete, the relationship itself will probably flounder.

How do excellent relationships contribute to the individuality of each partner? How does each self allow and encourage the other to be a self? What are the elements of relationships that work well?

Complementary sibling positions increase the odds that a relationship will require less effort to run smoothly. To some extent, all people are stuck in their sibling positions (and those of their parents) at the time they leave home. Their personality characteristics and reactivity patterns will have been partially determined by where they landed in the constellation of the family of origin and what their patterned emotional experience was in that family. Luckily, although these characteristics may seem to be set for life, with consistent effort they can change.

Even more important to a well-functioning relationship than sibling position and emotional patterns is one's level of differentiation. The higher the level, the less sibling position will be a factor in the success of a relationship.

Said another way, if two people with fortuitous sibling positions relate, the relationship may start out relatively problem-free. But whatever immaturity exists in either partner will spill out into other relationships where the sibling position may not be so fortuitous (such as at work or in child rearing). Those problem areas, as well as the fusion innate to the relationship itself, will ultimately come back to create anxiety for the two.

In any case, what it takes to improve a relationship is two people working to improve their own emotional functioning as autonomous selfs. The higher the level of functioning of each partner as an individual, the better the relationship works.

People with low levels of emotional maturity or differentiation attract other people with low maturity levels, and people with higher levels attract higher level people. Theoretically, in order for people to attract each other in the first place, they must be at exactly the same level of differentiation. That being the case, it is impossible to attach blame for relationship problems to one or the other partner. It is productive to look only at one's own contribution to the emotional challenges of the relationship.

Happily, although growth of self progresses slowly and differentiation probably changes but little over a lifetime, any change that one person makes in level of differentiation will eventually be matched by the other person. Even a small amount of change affects the relationship drastically.

At new, higher levels of personal differentiation, the ability to see process as it unfolds, as well as one's own part in that process, make it less likely for the relationship to get stuck in patterns or issues. At higher levels of differentiation, relationships serve whatever togetherness needs there may be, but since there are fewer togetherness needs, the two tend to function more as a harmonious team. Individuality is never lost in high level relationships. Rather, in and throughout all the teamwork, there exist two total and complete individuals, fully aware of self and the other, in open communication with each other. That is the ideal.

THE IDEAL—SEPARATE, EQUAL, AND OPEN

> The marriage is a functioning partnership. The spouses can enjoy the full range of emotional intimacy without either being de-selfed by the other. They can be autonomous selfs together or alone . . . . The differentiated person is always aware of others and the relationship system around him.
>
> **Murray Bowen, 1976**

It is probably safe to assume that a perfect relationship has never existed. Although elusive, ideals nevertheless are useful. Clinical experience has underscored the usefulness of clear thinking about the ideal—that is, the best possible—when people are working for better relationship functioning. Without an idea of what one is working towards, progress becomes difficult. Bowen's clear descriptions of functioning at high levels of differentiation have greatly facilitated functioning for many in relationships. An ideal relationship would be described much the same as an ideal self because, in reality, an ideal relationship is an equal, open relationship of two ideal selfs.

In an ideal relationship, then, there would be a greater degree of individuality and less togetherness—those basic, yet opposite human forces. Although relationships may seem to fulfill the togetherness force, there is less need for fusion or togetherness at high levels because there is less undifferentiation. So individuality is, surprisingly, more important to the success of the relationship. To the degree that each partner is an individual (emotionally differentiated from the other and from others in general), the relationship will be successful.

Here are a few of the characteristics of highly differentiated selfs and the relationship they would form: A "separate, equal, and open" relationship.

• Each is responsible for and only for self. It's not that they don't do things for each other; they may. But doing for the other is not carried to the point of doing the other in, or becoming frozen into the rut of an overfunctioning/underfunctioning pattern. Neither is dependent upon the other for happiness or emotional fulfillment. Happiness and emotional fulfillment are seen rather as responsibilities of the self, to be undertaken for the self. Being emotionally responsible must also include managing one's emotions so as not to burden the relationship with them. Emotional responsibility for self also involves not taking responsibility for the emotions of the other. While the relationship is not without sensitivity, there is no need to take responsibility for the other's emotions, since each is seen by the other as capable and responsible for that.

• The individuals are "in contact." They are present with one another a sufficient amount of the time and develop an understanding of personal meanings of each to the other. Neither speaks for the other but for and only for self.

• Each takes responsibility for defining, interpreting, and communicating his or her own thoughts and positions to the other. Conversely, no responsibility is taken for defining or communicating the thinking or positions of the other, since the other is seen as capable and adequate for that task.

• Awareness also marks the ideal relationship, arising automatically from increased differentiation. Gaining the ability to understand and take responsibility for one's own emotions requires developing an awareness of the emotional/feeling system that exists within the self. Accurate awareness of the emotions of other people grows out of the immense work of understanding and taking responsibility for one's own emotions. With time, this awareness is fine-tuned by experiential knowledge of the relationship, as it exists in the triangles of its broader system. The emotional system with its processes becomes predictable: "If I say 'X', I can predict his or her reaction might be 'Y.'"

Awareness is like the oil that keeps the relationship running smoothly and on course. It is born only out of a high degree of understanding of each individual of the self. Without understanding how the self operates emotionally, any attempt at awareness of the other is false, an invasion of the other's boundary for the purpose of borrowing functional self.

Of all the characteristics of an ideal relationship, that is, one that exists at high levels of differentiation, perhaps the three most imporant are:

- Separateness, emotionally, of the partners,
- Equality in their postures,
- Openness in communications.

A closer look at each of the three follows.

Separateness

> A more differentiated person can participate freely in the emotional sphere without the fear of becoming too fused with others. He or she also is free to shift to calm, logical reasoning for decisions that govern life.
>
> **Murray Bowen, 1976**

Partners in an ideal relationship lose no self into the relationship because their self boundaries are intact and their inner guidance systems are well developed. They do not take part in relationship fusions. They function as autonomous, individual selves in or out of the relationship. Neither relies on the other for "support," or expects the relationship to complete a part of the self perceived as lacking. Individuals at high levels of differentiation do not need support. Since a high level self is more fully developed, there is no need for completion. For this reason, it is possible for the emotional selfs of two high-level partners to retain a separateness not seen in most relationships. That is, each has a choice about whether to respond emotionally to the other's intensities. If two individuals are emotionally separate, any anxiety one may experience does not escalate into painful interchanges nor settle into emotional patterns.

In addition to being less emotionally reactive to each other, the partners, if emotionally separate, will have an ability to choose between emotions and thinking. This makes it possible for one partner to be calm in the face of the other's anxiety. If one of the two can stay calm and logical, anxiety does not escalate and become an emotional circuit.

This also means the relationship itself is not burdened with intense anxiety thrown into it by either self. Rather, each self is able to manage his or her own emotions adequately. After processing his or her own emotions, what each then contributes to the relationship is thoughtful and constructive.

If the boundaries of the self were completely intact, patterned relationships would not occur, since in patterns, borrowing and lending of self occurs.

What can an examination of the relationship patterns tell about boundaries?

• In the *conflict* pattern, each person in the relationship is absorbed in projecting blame and criticism on the other. Each invades the other's boundary. If focus on the self can be regained, the conflict will cease.

• The *overfunctioning/underfunctioning reciprocity* requires adapting by one self to the other to the point that one loses self and the other gains through leaky self-boundaries. In the constant demand for adaptation from the other, the one self gains more functional self than would be the case if the other were not so adaptive. By attempting to make a self out of two, the one appears to be doing well—but at the expense of the other. If boundaries had been maintained, self would neither be lost nor gained, and so great a degree of adaptation by one to the other would not be necessary or even possible.

• In the pattern of *distance*, the attempt to make a self out of two or more selfs usually starts out as intense closeness. The relationship defines the partners to such a degree that discomfort and eventually aversion to it develops. While distant relationships may appear to have intact boundaries, they do not. The distance is a reaction to the loss of self that has occurred in the original closeness. Had boundaries remained intact, there would have been no need for the distant posture.

• In the *triangling* pattern, there is an attempt to compensate for the distance that develops out of fusion by focusing emotional intensity toward a third self, in another fusion. If boundaries had been maintained, there would have been less fusing of selves in the first place and, therefore, less relationship anxiety. With less anxiety, there is less need for distance or the ensuing triangle. If people can work on the problem of boundaries between them, triangling will be less frequent and less intense.

Separateness of the selves is an important contribution to the excitement and pleasure of new relationships. Emotional fusion or relationship patterns have not become established, so the new relationship is free of the anxiety created by patterns and sparkles like fine crystal. If the emotional separateness of selves can be maintained over time, the relationship takes on a radiance that can be compared to that of a diamond.

Equality

> The basic self is not negotiable in the relationship system in that it is not changed by coercion or pressure, or to gain approval, or enhance one's stand with others.
>
> **Murray Bowen, 1972**

Since theoretically two people are not interested in spending time together unless they are at the same level of differentiation or emotional maturity, a basic equality of emotional maturity is present in any partnership. One might wonder, this being the case, how the overfunctioning/underfunctioning posture is able to occur. Even though levels of differentiation are equal, any partnership can have the effect of enhancing the functioning of one of the members, while compromising the functioning of the other. This results from the borrowing and lending of functional self. The partners end up with one doing better than the other, in unequal functioning postures.

The relationship posture of an ideal relationship is built upon the equality of the partners. In a high-level relationship, equality does not have to be worked at, it is just there. That equality is not based on tallying up individual assets; rather, it is a relationship stance, a posture assumed by the individuals. Each accepts the other as no more and no less talented, responsible, or free than him- or herself. Respect for the other, so often pointed to as essential for relationship success, is based on the equal posture. While equal partners certainly do things for each other and divide the labor or tasks of the relationship according to interests and ability, equality does not include patterned over- or underfunctioning.

Difficulties with people perceiving themselves and functioning as equals occur independently of gender. Problems of inequality probably have much more to do with how each has seen self and functioned for a very long time, than with gender, education, or social class. And while it is easy to blame the other for the inequality, each partner is actually playing an indispensable part in keeping the pattern alive. For that reason, either partner, seeing self as equal to the other, can change the situation.

When one is ready for an equal relationship, the principles of differentiation, thinking emotional systems, and seeing the process will point the way. To the extent that togetherness is not allowed to undo the individuality of each person, equality is not endangered. As one makes more progress toward becoming a complete and better-differentiated self, equality is less and less an issue in all relationships; there is less trading of selves into unequal postures. Keeping a constant focus on emotional process in relationships helps one know when one is beginning to take a posture that is less or more than equal. A relationship will not be fulfilling if either partner experiences self in the relationship as unequal to the other.

Openness

One of the most effective . . . mechanisms for reducing the overall level
of anxiety in a family is a relatively "open" relationship system. . . An
open relationship system, which is the opposite of an emotional cutoff, is one in which family members have a reasonable degree of
emotional contact with one another.

Murray Bowen, 1974

The complaint heard most frequently from couples seeking professional help is, "We have a communication problem!" Communication is an important and obvious part of any relationship. And
because communication is so noticeable to the people involved, it is
often seen as "the problem." However, to the extent that a relationship is involved in any of the relationship patterns, effective communication becomes impossible. When people work on the postures
underlying their communication problems, communication improves
almost automatically. Clearly, communication is less a problem than
a symptom: The problem is the relationship position itself.

Relationship postures are different from each other, and communication within each posture is correspondingly different. Although communication should not be mistaken for "the problem," a
great deal can be learned about communication by looking at how the
four different patterns affect communication. Conversely, by examining communication in a relationship, it's possible to identify the
underlying relationship positions.

The simplest form of relationship that exists is a feeling-emo-
tional relationship. This type of relationship, based more on feelings
and less on thought, is seen among animals, or very young children,
where thinking functions are only minimally present. There is a
simple give-and-take based mostly on the feeling states of the organisms. Many adults have not progressed far beyond this simple ebb
and flow of feelings and emotions, even though their thinking brain

is fully developed. In every relationship, emotions are continuously signalled and received nonverbally. Facial expressions, physical postures, and gestures are constantly being transmitted and understood in any significant relationship. Reactivity can thus be instantly stimulated, even though it is not translated into thought or words by either party.

To move a relationship past the simple emotional level, verbal communication is necessary. Verbal communication of the thoughtful part of each self to the other is another important hallmark of high-level relationships. In the act of verbal expression, the emotional separation of the selfs is expressed or explained and furthered at the same time. It is one thing to be a self. It is another to define that self to the other(s) in a relationship or a relationship system, a necessary component of being a self. Communication at higher levels of differentiation then becomes a self-defining give and take of ideas.

In relationship patterns, the give and take of ideas between partners is stunted or distorted to the degree that a pattern is in place. Anxiety generated by the fusion that is expressed in the pattern interferes with thinking. In the distancing pattern, for example, communication is severely restricted. This is not to say, of course, that the partners are not interacting. There is an emotional arousal between them and interaction occurs. But the interaction is on a reactive basis, and this reactivity serves only to restrict communication further. Of course, it is possible for a distanced couple to appear to be open in communication, talking much but saying nothing really important to each other, carefully avoiding meaningful issues. Often such a couple is unaware of the true distance because it is so carefully disguised by empty chatter. So, in distancing there is less and less relevant communication; in time there may be none. There may be complete cutoff of verbal communication long before actual emotional cutoff occurs.

In optimal communication, then, people are open to talk, and they must talk about relevant matters. What can be learned about optimal communication from the other relationship patterns?

In the conflictual relationship pattern, there is also a great deal of emotional triggering of each by the other and transfer of emotion from each to the other. Each projects blame on the other. Because of the emotional triggering value of these behaviors, clear-headed thoughtfulness becomes impossible. Rather each becomes embroiled in a frenzied attempt to transfer emotional reactivity to the other. Since each is preoccupied with the other, thoughtful focus on the self is missing. Blaming, accusative "You . . ." assertions violate each other's boundaries. Calm, thoughtful "I think . . ." statements are missing.

Communication of ideas is dependent upon an emotionally calm brain state for reliable thought production. In conflict, there is a great deal of interaction and what might even pass for communication of ideas. But "thinking" is so emotionally based in conflict that what is really shared is emotion and not ideas that the partners would stand by or defend over time. Therefore, a second characteristic of optimal communication becomes clear: It is nonreactive.

Triangling, whether it be through a child or another adult, effectively stifles the flow of ideas between two people who are significant to each other. Ideas may be generated, but they are about, to, or through the third party. Since the partners make contact primarily around or through the third party, the verbal communications are completely taken up with that third person.

For example, in the case of a symptomatic child, nearly all of the parents' conversations and thinking may be taken up with worry and concern over the child. They can be seen to give advice and directives to him or her almost continuously. In the case of a triangled adult, such as in an affair, optimal communication between the primary two is impossible because the emotional reactivity engendered prevents thoughtfulness. In addition, because the two are not communicating, *with* each other *about* the relationship, they are communicating via someone else. So a third essential of communication is directness. The partners must talk to and with each other about each other.

In an overfunctioning/underfunctioning reciprocity, the communications style is one of the most symptomatic characteristics and may easily be taken as the problem. One of the partners is "the sayer" and the other "the listener." Verbal communications stay one-way for the most part. The overfunctioner takes the part of chief communicator, with communications taking the forms of telling, advising, preaching, teaching, or explaining.

It is clear that a fourth characteristic of communicating well must be mutuality. A measure of mutuality might be that each partner speaks and listens about an equal amount of time, over time. Another measure would be the degree to which people can talk to each other while remaining responsible only for self and the communication of self's own ideas.

In reality, it is surprising how often couples will describe many years of their relationship as "good" or "satisfying" to both parties, even though careful history-taking reveals optimal communication to have been sadly lacking all the while. This phenomenon illustrates how effective patterns in an emotional system can be at calming anxiety. The relationship patterns, along with their ineffective communication styles, can serve to maintain an equilibrium for many years.

From examining the four relationship postures, then, a description of the elements of optimal communication in an emotionally significant relationship can be derived. It is the direct, verbal, mutual, and nonreactive give and take of relevant ideas.

This kind of communication is the expression of a high-level relationship, and it facilitates attainment of an even better-functioning relationship. While it is possible to see that communications are symptomatic of the relationship patterns, they also exert an effect of their own upon the relationship, so they are well worth working at.

Listening is fifty percent of the communication process in an ideal relationship. Listening is active. The best listeners seem to have an ability to mentally "get in the skin" of the other, yet keep utterly calm and quiet so as to better understand what is said. (They can also quickly get back out and into their own skin.) It is impossible to have high-level communication unless both partners are skilled listeners, and it is probably as difficult to learn to be a good listener as it is to be a clear, direct, nonreactive talker. On the average, it takes therapists at least a year of training experience to become adequate listeners.

An important part of listening is the ability to separate the anxiety of the speaker from what is being said. Anxiety on the part of the speaker produces interference in the listener. Thus, when speaking, it is important to address the listener in a way that communicates or can be heard. Communication in general will reach a higher level if personal anxiety can be processed before communication is undertaken. Insistence upon continual "dumping" of anxiety into the relationship is a destructive pattern. When one can take responsibility for one's own anxiety and the processing of it, communication will be much better.

Storytelling is an excellent technique for getting oneself heard. Storytelling comes naturally to many people. Others must work to become good storytellers. The ability to spin an interesting yarn is a wonderful asset in relationships. Stories, creative, and colorful, can be overused, but they can often make a lasting point without de-selfing anyone.

At the high levels of relationship functioning, it could be postulated that communication would have certain further characteristics, growing out of the high level of differentiation of the partners. Here is a partial list for starters.

Thinking-based conversation. Because each person is responsible for and is processing his or her own feelings, communications are free of emotionally driven tangentiality—that is, getting off the point. It becomes possible for each to think all the way through a problem or topic in the presence of the other, with each tracking the thought processes of the other accurately. Less emotional triggering of one by the other makes this thoughtful tracking possible. Each, under these circumstances, is more able to accurately define and express his or her best thinking on the subject. The best thinking is guided by the principles of the basic self.

Creativity. When a mutual thinking-through process operates, the thinking of each is stimulated by the thinking of the other so the partnership exerts a positive influence on each member. While most thinking is probably still done alone, much creative thinking may actually be done with each other.

Self-definition. High-level partners can use thinking-based communication as a self-defining process, even though they don't need another person for the work of defining self. Explaining one's thoughts to another or accurately hearing the thinking of another can be a rigorous exercise in defining of self. One's stands on issues, one's ideas, and one's beliefs all come into clear focus during such a process. Learning to only define self to another in this context will take the "you," which usually invades boundaries, out of most communications. Instead, communication will be done from the "I think . . ." or "It seems to me . . ." point of view.

Meaningfulness. When two people experience each other as separate selves and as equals, they are free to communicate accurately their definitions of self to the other. This includes where they stand on issues. They also are freer to communicate completely, because they are relieved of emotional consequences. With process issues worked through, they can trust each other not to react emotionally to a given communication but to think instead. Such communication imparts a sense of meaning to the relationship and, indeed, to the lives of the partners.

In aspiring to ideal relationships, the three components—emotional separateness, equality, and open communication—for most people, remain goals. The effort to understand each of the three goals separately leads, surprisingly, to the discovery of their great degree of interdependence. The more familiar one becomes with them, the more one realizes the ideas of separateness, equality, and openness can scarcely be teased apart.

For example, if one thinks at length about emotional separateness and all its implications, one is inevitably led to equality and open communication. Or, as we have seen, it becomes impossible to consider openness in communication without the ideas of equality and emotional separateness entering in. The interdependence is not merely a theoretical phenomenon: Working on one component of relationships elevates all the others.

Figure 11. A separate, equal, and open relationship.

As people work toward differentiation of self, thinking systems, and watching for emotional process while they work, their relationship functioning improves steadily.

An understanding of theory and a glimpse of the ideal makes it possible to take the further step into the work that brings theory to life.

III

Toward Better Relationships

Toward Better Relationships

The goal is . . . to take a microscopic step toward a better level of
differentiation, in spite of the togetherness forces that oppose.

Murray Bowen, 1976

Excellence in relationships, for most people, ranks alongside unified
field theory among the inscrutable problems of the world. That may
be because what it takes to make a truly successful relationship is two
people operating at high levels of differentiation. Most people work
with only modest levels of differentiation. Emotional immaturity
carries with it chronic anxiety, which, when expressed in relationships, wreaks havoc.

Since, theoretically, two people are not attracted to each other
unless they are on the same level of differentiation, each person, if the
relationship is not going well, contributes his or her 50 percent to the
problem. Therefore, if either person in a relationship increases his or
her own level of emotional maturity, the relationship will gradually
improve. The improvement will be uneven because partners improve
their functioning at different times. Typically, one partner starts the
process by improving functioning or taking a stand for self in the
relationship. Then the initiating partner coasts for a time. While the
first is coasting, the other begins to work on functioning. It is virtually
impossible to relate closely to a person who is differentiating a self
(increasing his or her level of basic self) and not do the same oneself.

Another way of stating this is as follows: In a relationship that
is not working well, two or more selves have been emotionally
fused—an inherently painful state of affairs. For each partner, in

short, there is a lack of intactness of the boundaries of the basic self. Self is too easily lost or taken on. In order to remedy this situation, a responsible stance must be taken; self boundaries must be defined. If one begins to work on differentiating a self, the other will eventually adjust by joining the first at the new, higher level of differentiation.

The relationship usually goes through predictable stages when one person begins to work on differentiating a self from the togetherness of the relationship. In the words of Bowen, "*The family system is . . . disturbed when any family member moves toward a slightly higher level of differentiation, and it will move automatically to restore the family system to its former equilibrium. Thus, any small step toward differentiation is accompanied by a small emotional upheaval in the family system. This pattern is so predictable that absence of an emotional reaction is good evidence that the differentiating effort was not successful. There are three predictable steps in the family reaction to differentiation. They are: (1) 'You are wrong' or some version of that; (2) 'Change back,' which can be communicated in many different ways, and (3) 'If you do not, these are the consequences.' If the differentiating one can stay on course without defending self or counterattacking, the emotional reaction is usually brief and the other then expresses appreciation in some way.*"

He continues, "*The clearest examples of the steps in differentiation occur in family psychotherapy with husband and wife. The following is a typical example. One couple in family therapy spent several months on issues about the togetherness in the marriage. They discussed meeting the needs of each other; attaining a warm, loving relationship; the ways each disappointed the other; and the making of joint decisions. They discovered new differences in opinion as the process continued.*

"*Then the husband spent a few weeks thinking about himself, his career, and where he stood on some central issues between him and his wife. His focus on himself stirred an emotional reaction in the wife. Her anxiety episode lasted about a week as she begged him to return to the togetherness and then went into a tearful, angry, emotional attack in which she accused him of being selfish, self-centered, incapable of loving anyone, and an inadequate husband. She was sure the only answer was divorce. He maintained his calm and was able to stay close to her.*

"The following day, the relationship was calm. At the next therapy session she said to her husband, 'I liked what you were doing, but it made me mad. I wanted to control what I was saying, but it had to come out. All the time I was watching you, hoping you would not give in. I am so glad you did not let me change you.' They were on a new and less intense level of togetherness which was followed by the wife starting on a self-determined course, with the husband then reacting emotionally to her efforts at differentiation.

"In this example, the husband's effort represented a small step toward a better level of differentiation. Had he yielded to her demand, or attacked, he would have slipped back to her level. When he held his position, her emotional reaction represented a pull up to his level. This theoretical orientation considers this sequence a basic increase in bilateral differentiation which can never return to the former level. On the new level they both have different attitudes about togetherness and individuality. They say things like, 'We are much more separate but we are closer. The old love is gone. I miss it sometimes, but the new love is calmer and better. I know it sounds crazy, but that's how it is.'"

Thus, relationship work, paradoxically, is a solitary project. It may feel like growing a self. It is not necessary, important, or even possible to work on the other person. One cannot change another person, though the temptation to try is always there. Change must come from within the self, for one's own reasons. Differentiation in the other may be stimulated by one's own efforts to differentiate a self, but the other cannot be encouraged, prodded, or advised in this respect. The impetus must come solely from within the self.

Many people characterize their relationship as being like a roller coaster—subject to extreme highs, predictably followed by extreme lows.

Figure 12. Many relationships are characterized by constant predictable rounds of ups and downs.

The work one does on the self will tend to smooth out the highs and lows. Like a perfect golf swing, a smooth-running relationship takes both mental work and field practice. It doesn't matter who begins the work on self; the other will usually respond in kind, given time. It is irresponsible to say, "Why do I have to do all the work?" Of course, one has to do all the work on the self, and relationship improvements spring from that source: It takes two to fuse but only one to begin unraveling the threads of lost self entangled with the other.

GROWING A SELF

The individuality force emerges slowly at first, and it takes very little togetherness force to drive it back underground for fairly long periods.

Murray Bowen, 1975

The best relationships are enjoyed by people with a high degree of differentiation of self. This means, as stated earlier, that they have a well-developed basic self. As we have seen, highly differentiated people show, above all else, two prominent attributes: Well-defined self boundaries and a well-developed thinking inner guidance system.

The thinking inner guidance system, a part of basic self, is the part on which motivation is founded and decisions and judgments are based. People at higher levels of differentiation are comfortable with their own well-thought-out beliefs, standards, values, and priorities. This is not to say their beliefs, values, or priorities might not change over time. Rather, at any given time, they have a fairly clear idea of what they believe and why they believe it. They can keep their minds open to new data and have the ability to change based on the new information. This characteristic makes it possible to live a principled life. A life lived according to the principles of a thought-out inner guidance system has an entirely different quality, course, and outcome than a life lived according to principles implicitly or explicitly set by one's environment. This characteristic is what makes it possible for one to say "no" when that becomes appropriate. In other words, the effort toward differentiation frees one from trying to be what one thinks others want one to be, yet it allows one to remain in open contact with significant others in the emotional system.

The inner guidance system of well-differentiated individuals make it possible for them to be less concerned about what people think of them, whether or not they are loved, and how they appear to other people. As mature adults, they no longer need parents or parental love, so they don't have to spend their lives seeking nurturing from others. This fact relieves relationships of a great deal of pressure often put on them.

The well-developed and well-defined self boundaries of people at high levels of differentiation mean they are neither borrowers nor lenders of self. They do not lose self into a relationship, and they do not need to borrow self from someone else in order to function. To determine whether a significant amount of self has been lost into the relationship, an important question to ask is: "How much time do I spend thinking about myself and my life course, rather than about the other person, the relationship, or a triangled third?"

Further, emotionally mature or highly differentiated people have a well-developed ability to choose between the thinking and feeling systems. The importance of this ability cannot be overstressed, for when emotions are aroused, clear thinking is impossible. It is characteristic of the feeling system that feelings come and go swiftly; they are evanescent. If one bases a life course on feelings, that life will be marked by ups and downs, tangents, and lack of direction. If anxious feelings can be calmed at will, productive thoughtfulness will take over. Most of us need all the calm thoughtfulness we can bring to bear on life's problems—both individual problems and relationship problems.

With an improved ability to choose between the thinking and the feeling systems, one becomes less reactive to the emotions of the other person and to stresses outside the relationship. On reaching this point, one has improved emotional maturity and thereby, relationships.

Differentiating a self in one's family of origin

> I believe that the level of differentiation of a person is largely deter-
> mined by the time he leaves the parental family and he attempts a life
> of his own. Thereafter, he tends to replicate the lifestyle from the
> parental family in all future relationships. It is not possible ever to
> make more than minor changes in one's basic level of self; but from
> clinical experience I can say it is possible to make slow changes, and
> each small change results in the new "world" of a different lifestyle. As
> I see it now, the critical stage is passed when the individual can begin
> to know the difference between emotional functioning and intellectual
> functioning, and when he has developed ways for using the knowledge
> for solving future problems in a lifelong effort of his own.
>
> **Murray Bowen, 1976**

> I have suggested to people, "If you can get a one-to-one relationship
> with each living person in your extended family, it will help you 'grow
> up' more than anything else you could ever do in life."

> There were comments, such as, "Family-systems theory is just another
> theory until you see it work with your own family."
>
> **Murray Bowen, 1975**

How does one go about becoming one of those people who seems to
attract and maintain smooth relationships? That is, how does one go
about differentiating more self? If it is true that one's relationships are
only as good as one's self-knowledge, understanding, and self-
regulation, then how does one go about improving on those?

If there is a high road toward improving one's relationships, it
is working toward improving those in one's family of origin. In fact,
it appears that only limited improvement of other relationships is
possible without work in the family of origin. The family one grew up
in is the best of all possible places to learn about oneself. There are
many reasons for this. One is that the lack of self (or the tendency to
borrow and lend self) exhibited in relationships dates back to the

early years spent in the first family. Whatever amount of self (emotional maturity or differentiation) one has been able to develop at the time of leaving that family is the amount of self carried into adulthood. So the problem for everyone is very old.

The same process was operating in one's parents and in their parents before them; a lack of self (immaturity, attachment, or undifferentiation) gets passed down from generation to generation. In order to increase personal maturity, then, it is most useful to understand the emotional system that exists among the members of one's extended family, by relating to it and by teaching oneself to get out of the emotional patterns reverberating in it. One gains understanding of the self to the degree that one understands the family system that one grew up in.

The most difficult impasses usually occur in the triangle with one's mother and father. Teaching about differentiation of self, Bowen pointed out it is especially important to get an individual relationship with each parent. One parent may be the spokesperson, and so it may be easier to get a relationship with that one. As soon as one has resolved the intensity with one parent, it is important to do the same with the other. A goal is to be able to relate to parents, as an open and separate equal, personal things about yourself and them, without going into a lot of extraneous issues and without getting into criticism or sermonizing.

At family gatherings, a goal becomes to spend as much individual time with each person as possible. Returning to the family of origin often is necessary to learn the patterns of how the family system operates, how it functions emotionally, and how to control oneself in it. Eventually one gets to the neutral position where "They don't love me" is irrelevant, and one can understand from the inside that they were doing the best they knew.

Caution is necessary: Many people have heard Bowen's idea of going back home, but they forget the goals for going there and the principles for how to conduct themselves when they get there. Too many people go back home and make accusations, participate in confrontations, or attempt to do therapy that only ends in more intense family emotional processes (and often in cutoff). In some cases, families have been virtually blown apart by attempts to work on the others instead of the self.

The process becomes a lifelong project for most people who begin it, and it often follows several predictable steps that are repeated over and over again. The following is a brief summary of what usually takes place over years in the effort to differentiate more of a self in one's family of origin.

A useful beginning in such a process is to try to develop a one-to-one relationship with every person in one's family of origin, becoming aware of and working through the triangles, conflict, distancing, or overfunctioning/underfunctioning patterns that are in place or that develop. Where there are cutoffs, the goal becomes simply to get back into contact. Of course, rarely does one stay out of all the family patterns and emotional intensities; one is very much a part of these or this work would not be necessary. But with a thoughtful approach, hard work, and often professional coaching, in time one does better at "staying out" emotionally while staying in contact with each person in the system.

Next, after making contact, it may be useful to step back and observe the emotional processes and patterned emotional behaviors in the family. The best results come from staying emotionally calm so that one can see as objectively as possible what emotional patterns occur in the family, as well as what triggers them. People sometimes think of the calm, objective attitude of a scientist. In this way, one might "see," perhaps for the first time, patterns that have been present in the family for generations. With cutoff, for example, the observation phase will help one understand, at least to some degree, the nature of the reactivity that made the cutoff necessary and kept it in place.

After seeing how emotions are processed in one's family, a thoughtful plan can be made as to how to relate to that emotional system in a more mature way. This thoughtful planning is crucial to one's success. Without it, one will simply play the same role one always has in the family emotional patterns and processes. With careful thinking and planning, and even rehearsing, one can learn to play one's own part in the patterns differently.

Playing one's part in the old family patterns differently is the important next step. That is, in interactions with members of the family, one makes the effort to respond calmly, as planned and rehearsed, when the old emotional patterns begin to snap into their accustomed places. As difficult as it is to understand one's own family emotional process, it is still more difficult to change one's emotional way of being in that family. These ways of being have had years of repetition and rehearsal. All the members of the cast are in their respective roles, and they work together automatically toward a predetermined outcome. The sheer difficulty of this kind of work may be a factor in explaining the life changes seen when the work is successfully undertaken.

The most difficult and somewhat predictable part of differentiation of self in one's family is managing oneself around the family system's reaction to the change. When one does not play the accustomed role in the emotional pattern, or when one takes a step out of the family emotional system, the system will react with various intense expressions of emotion. These may take the form of threats or criticism. Intensity may increase in the family triangles. However, if one works at staying in calm contact with various family members, continuing to relate to the family, without reacting to their emotional reactions, those reactions will subside. Now the differentiating person becomes aware of a higher level of individual functioning.

Later, the differentiating one is often accorded a different position in the family. And the rewarding observation is often made that various other family members will show evidence of having joined the differentiating one at a higher level of functioning also.

If this process is repeated many times, relationships between the differentiating one and the family will improve, and other relationships will also improve for the differentiating one. Changing the patterned ways of reacting and moving within one's family is such hard work that when any progress is made, the basic self emerges fundamentally changed. It is possible to see progress in this work: More neutrality and less reactivity will have been attained when one can listen to people without defending or attacking them, avoiding confrontations and showdowns.

The project will be more effective if one can learn about the individuals who peopled the generations of one's family. It is surprising how much can be learned about relatives who are long gone. A family diagram is very useful here. Such a diagram not only places each individual in a nuclear family but also charts important facts, such as locations, educational achievement, health status, and occupation. Dates of births, moves, deaths, and immigration are all recorded on the family diagram. Thus, the diagram becomes an important document, summarizing a great deal of information. (See diagram on page 124).

After the information is recorded, emotional facts regarding family members and relationship patterns in nuclear families can be sought, often from older living members of the family. Stories told by these people as well as by family friends may reveal trends, such as themes passed down through the family—themes of achievement, conflict, distance, violence, or cutoff. Relationship patterns among family members may eventually be seen through this kind of detective work, all of which adds life and breath to the bones of the family diagram.

If the goal is to know self and work with one's own patterns, the highest yield comes from going back to the extended family alone, without other family members. If the reactivity with mother and father is too great, it is possible to postpone working on differentiation there for a while, and go to the families from which they came, learning what one can about their parents and siblings, as well as their families. This effort will be extremely worthwhile. If these people are dead, it is sometimes possible to find people who were emotionally important to parents. One's mother's best friend, for example, might have been an important part of her emotional field and could provide helpful information.

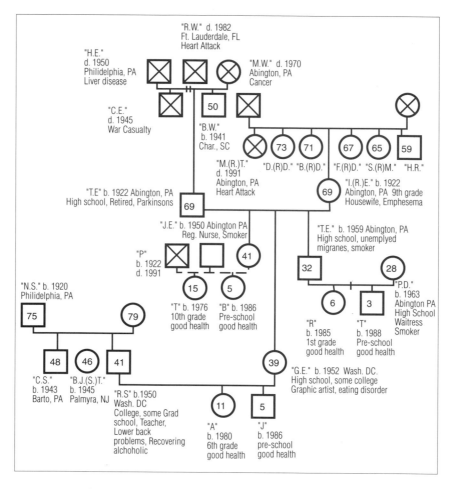

Fig. 13. Multigenerational family diagram.

At times people are in a cut-off position and, though they can see benefits from this kind of effort, are blocked. Old grudges, hurts, or feeling patterns impede progress. A knowledge of family systems theory helps get past this. The current cutoff is only this generation's version of a family tendency toward cutoff that may go back many generations. If one can get past that family tendency to cutoff when the going gets rough, there will not only be a fundamental change in the self, but the cutoff tendency will be modified for the next generation.

As one makes contact with one's family system, while thinking systems—seeing as much of the total complex picture as one can—cause-and-effect thinking, blame, and criticism drop off. The biggest picture one can possibly get will usually lead to a growing acceptance of all the members of the family. This acceptance, which grows out of the wide-lens view, is neither critical nor competitive.

It is important to remember that working to differentiate a self in one's family of origin is not doing therapy on the family, nor is it family sensitivity training, nor is it talking over issues. It does not entail rehashing past slights, grudges, or deficiencies. It is not "sharing," much less dumping, one's feelings. Rather, with focus mostly on the self instead of the others, it is moving to a different level of comfort and responsibility in one's own family. It may not involve much talk at all in some families. In others it may. In its simplest terms, *efforts at differentiation amount to becoming a better version of oneself in one's family-of-origin relationships.*

Different tactics must be employed in peaceful, agreeable families than in explosive families. In a peaceful family, one sometimes must get emotions stirred up in order to see the triangles and emotional process. If this strategy is used in a more emotionally intense family, however, one courts disaster.

Work on the self *vis a vis* one's family of origin usually becomes, for those who take it on, a profound adventure that carries with it a life-changing effect. Clinical evidence is mounting that changing one's relationships with the people one grew up with exerts a much more powerful effect on the self than simply talking about these relationships in a therapist's office. Many who have taken up this challenge report it to be a rewarding and worthwhile endeavor, not only in developing individual strengths but also in functioning better in all relationships.

MANAGING THE EMOTIONAL SELF

IN RELATIONSHIPS

The instinctual force toward differentiation is built into the organism, just as are the emotional forces that oppose it.

Murray Bowen, 1976

It is reasonably accurate to compare the functioning of the emotional and intellectual systems to the structure and function of the brain.

Murray Bowen, 1976

If it is only the self that one has a chance of influencing, how does one manage the self when relationship issues arise? What does it mean to manage one's emotional self in relationships?

Until now it has been emphasized that issues of managing the self can be brought into therapy and solved there. For example, if one experienced strong feelings toward the therapist that were based in older relationships (transference), they could be worked out in therapy. This effort was thought to influence personality patterns in all relationships.

In the new theory, if strong feelings arise toward the therapist or other people that are based in old relationships, they are best dealt with in the original family emotional system where they developed. If issues arise in relationships, they are dealt with there. Partners manage themselves in the context of the relationship situation (not in therapy), always working to bring themselves to emotional neutrality around issues.

One important aid to improving emotional self-management, besides working to differentiate a self in one's original family, is self-regulation training.

Training in Self-Regulation

> It is impossible for there to be more than relative separation between emotional and intellectual functioning, but those whose intellectual functioning can retain relative autonomy in periods of stress are more flexible, more adaptable, and more independent of the emotionality about them. They cope better with life stresses, their life courses are more orderly and successful, and they are remarkably free of human problems.
>
> **Murray Bowen, 1976**

> Every change in the physiological state is accompanied by an appropriate change in the mental-emotional state . . . and conversely, every change in the mental-emotional state . . . is accompanied by an appropriate change in the physiological state.
>
> **Elmer Green, 1969**

Self-knowledge is the *sine qua non* out of which high-level relationship skills develop. That is, if one will pay close attention to the self and one's reactivity at every level possible, one will be able to develop a degree of mastery of a factual base that applies to all one's relationship systems. Yogis, of course, have been interested in and have practiced the control of automatic body functions as a spiritual discipline for thousands of years.

Combining concepts derived from hypnosis, medical research, and logic methods, Johannes Schultz, in 1910, developed a system of self-regulation he called Autogenic Training—that is, self-generated or self-willed training. He recommended six exercises. They were: induction of heaviness, peripheral warmth, heart rate regulation, respiratory control, abdominal warmth, and cooling of the forehead. With these exercises, he obtained a measure of control over changes in attention, consciousness, thought, and emotion.

With modern technology, instruments can be attached to various parts of the body, giving feedback regarding physiologic change to consciousness. This makes it possible for a subject to learn these exercises in a much shorter amount of time. Whenever involuntary processes can be brought to consciousness, learning is greatly facilitated. On the cutting edge of behavioral science today, the development of biofeedback offers a means of training so that what appeared to be inflexible, automatic responses can be modified.

Since muscular relaxation is incompatible with anxiety, biofeedback training becomes a way to get a little better at increasing one's power of choice between feeling and thought. It is a way of breaking into one's emotional and physiological patterns and changing their direction, giving greater flexibility in one's reactions. Since so much of relationship distress comes out of inadequately processed and managed anxiety, any tool that will aid in the management of anxiety will automatically enhance a relationship.

Presently, the three major areas of biofeedback training are (1) reduction of striated muscle tension, (2) training to increase temperature in the skin, and (3) increasing the percentage of alpha rhythm in the EEG record, which measures electrical wave patterns of the brain. Others are being developed and may be available in the future.

Drs. Elmer E. Green and Alyce M. Green of the Menninger Clinic tell the following story about skin-temperature training, which is fairly typical for people who use biofeedback training: "It seems to us that a psychotherapeutic component is associated with almost every use of temperature training, and we hope this observation will be fully researched. It is not possible for a patient to realize that normally involuntary processes of the body can be controlled to some extent, without at the same time undergoing a modification of self-image. This was first brought forcibly to our attention in 1970 when a member of the Board of Trustees of the Menninger Foundation was a demonstration subject in a Science Day program. He was given autogenic phrases to use in front of a group of trustees while attached to a temperature feedback machine. At the phrase, 'My hands are warm,' his temperature began to drop, decreasing by several degrees in a few minutes. The subject was not aware of this decrease until we asked him at the end of the session what feelings he had experienced during the session. He replied that his fingers had begun to tingle, and that reminded him of an exercise in self-hypnosis he had practiced several years previously, learning to make his fingers tingle. 'So this was warmth,' he thought, and he 'really made them tingle.' It was explained that he had made a mistake, that in his case tingling meant cooling, but the fact that the temperature had dropped was of no consequence in the demonstration. The significance lay in the fact that he was the one who had done it.

"Two months later he surprised us by writing and saying that the fifteen-minute demonstration was one of the most important events in his life. Until then, he said, he had not really believed he could control anything, but in the last two months he was able to lose 12 pounds and now was able to clear all the correspondence off his desk in the first hour each morning, something he had not been able to do previously. This type of change in self-image is not uncommon in biofeedback trainees, though sometimes it might not be noticeable for several weeks. With many patients, as in the example above, temperature training serves to help reorganize their lives, not because it is necessarily good to have warm hands but because of the feeling of self-mastery they get. That feeling, if it could be put in mathematical terms, would be called 'an enabling function.' It enables the patient to take positive action in a variety of ways. In other words, the gains from temperature training as well as from other kinds of feedback training, are not merely physical."

The Greens go on to tell of other ways that the training may be working to produce change in general:

"After a bad psychophysiological habit is consciously replaced with a good habit, it need not remain in the forefront of consciousness. Everyone knows this is true in the striate domain, as when we learn to drive a car or play a musical instrument, but it is also true in the autonomic domain. When a more relaxed, poised, alert, sensitive way of life becomes habitual, it no longer needs to be consciously practiced. It literally becomes a way of life. This is the goal of our training program for the patients, whatever their problem, and the number of successes makes the game worthwhile."

"Striate" refers to muscles normally under voluntary control: that is, striate muscles (so-called because they have stripes when seen under the microscope) work on command of the will. The system of striate muscles is considered to be fairly easily trainable, as for example in athletics. The autonomic or involuntary nervous system, on the other hand, ordinarily has nothing to do with voluntary control. It makes automatic adjustments of organs such as the heart, blood vessels, and bronchial tubes, all of which have "smooth" muscles, also so-called because of their microscopic appearance.

Until recently, it was believed that the autonomic nervous system was not controllable voluntarily, except perhaps by certain yogis. Biofeedback technology, because it brings into consciousness processes normally unavailable to conscious monitoring, makes it possible for almost anyone to learn to control and modify automatic reactions.

Biofeedback training is a powerful tool for learning to choose between feelings and emotions. At special times of stress for a relationship or for the self, autogenic training can make a great difference in one's ability to handle life crises well. Not only does the training make a difference in the ability to give one's self more comfort at will, but also because of the ability to calm anxiety, it makes it possible to think more clearly so appropriate action can be taken. The evidence for relationship systems such as nuclear families operating as an emotional unit is inescapable in the biofeedback laboratory. There whole families can be monitored together. It becomes possible to see how an emotion travels through the group. More and more, it is being seen how the physiologies of individuals in relationship postures and triangles are inextricably linked.

The ability to remain relaxed at will also means one is able to remain calm and thoughtful when one's partner is anxious. Remaining calm in the presence of another's anxiety saves many a situation from escalating to the crisis point. Further, the ability to choose emotions and physiology, to control anxiety as one challenges one's patterns of reactivity, defines self-boundaries. Self-control is a hallmark of all separate-but-equal, well-functioning relationships.

Fifteen people struggled with addictions to prescription tranquilizers and sleeping medications. Their addicted behavior was understood in the context of relationship postures and anxiety. They were, without exception, in an underfunctioning position in their significant relationships. The relationship anxiety, however, was magnified several times by the intense anxiety that was a symptom of withdrawal from the medications. Of the fifteen, three took advantage of biofeedback relaxation training to help with the withdrawal.

The three stood out from the group in several ways: They made many fewer panicky calls to the consultant. They experienced the same anxiety of withdrawal as the rest of the group but, using the new responses they had learned in their training, were able to calm the anxiety without resorting to medication. Best of all, they reported that, as they gained control of their feeling states through the use of biofeedback training, they were able to function more as equals in their relationships. In this way they worked directly on the root of the problem that led to addiction in the first place.

How does relaxation training in particular improve relationship functioning? These addicted people described that at those moments when relationship patterns snapped into place, carrying their attendant anxiety, the voluntary muscular system tensed up and further fed the anxiety. But the relaxation response interfered with the anxiety. With anxiety lowered, people could keep thinking. The ability to think in an anxious relationship field made it possible to be more of a self in their relationships.

Mr. M explains, "When my boss comes at me tense and demanding I'm able more of the time now to go into my relaxation mode. Maybe not at the exact moment he is coming at me, but usually very soon afterwards, I'm able to. I can think about what is an appropriate response from me, what I can do, and what I can't. I can approach him with a calm manner and an answer that is thought out. He becomes reasonable, which surprises me—I mean, the way one person being calm can affect the mood of the other person. The same thing has been true with my girlfriend. When she begins to plan my life, I can now back off mentally, relax a little, and, instead of just going into shutdown, keep thinking. I can decide what it is I think and what I want to do or not do and why, and then give her my input. She actually seems to appreciate my being more active in the relationship. She is getting the idea now, too. When I slip back into my old pattern and ask her for advice that I don't really need, she usually makes a joke that lets me know she is thinking about relationship patterns, trying to stay out of them!"

Although biofeedback training has had powerful effects on self-growth and certainly influences relationships in a positive way, it has been studied even more thoroughly in relation to several illnesses. Asthma, high blood pressure, and headaches are well-documented physical conditions that often respond favorably to biofeedback training. Diabetes is now being studied with encouraging results. Alpha wave training is being used to increase creativity.

Biofeedback shows us incredibly more than we have known before about the interplay between emotions, physiology, and relationships. In addition to providing that knowledge, it is becoming a powerful new tool in modifying that interplay.

PROCESSING FEELINGS AND
DEALING WITH CRISIS

The term reflex is accurate in that it occurs automatically and out of awareness, but like a reflex emotions can be brought within limited observation and under limited conscious control, just as one can control a knee jerk with specific energy.

Murray Bowen, 1973

Since Freud, therapists have had one answer to the question, "What do I do with these feelings?" The answer has been: "Talk it out." Certainly it works in the consulting room. If one can talk it out with a professional listener, one usually will leave the room feeling better.

The problem is that the attempt to manage feelings outside the consulting room—in relationships—by talking out all feelings, often burdens the relationship with more emotional intensity than it can bear. Certainly there may be times when it is appropriate to process feelings in a relationship. However, if relationships are the court of first resort for feelings, the relationships most often run into trouble.

Perhaps feelings are best processed by the individual in his or her own head. This gives new meaning to taking responsibility for one's feelings. How exactly does one process a feeling reaction? The process probably has at least several steps.

1. Observing the feeling state: Step away mentally to see and feel what is going on inside. Where in the body is the hurt or tension?

2. Calming the feelings as soon as possible. "As soon as possible" may be only after a good cry, but as soon as a feeling is located physically, let it go physically. Don't prolong any emotional intensity. Taking a few slow, deep breaths, relaxing muscles, or exercising

may help get a calm feeling state. Often people stop working once they are calm, but ideally, that is when the work begins. Once one is calm, one can think.

3. Thinking:
   A. What is the feeling that has been triggered?
   B. What was the trigger? A help in determining this is placing the onset of the anxiety in time: When did it begin? Just before the onset of the anxiety, what was happening? Using this rather meticulous approach, one can identify the trigger.
   C. Is this a trigger/feeling response that has been experienced before—in other words, is it a pattern? If so, what is this feeling pattern about? Rejection? Competition? Someone from the past who reacted this way? In other words, is it a repetition reaction?
   D. Is this an appropriate response for an adult at this time, given this particular trigger circumstance?
   E. If this is not a desired response:

4. Are there other options? What are they? Rehearsing these other options in the head is useful.

5. Repetition of the new response in real life as well as in the head frequently helps it become a more automatic response. Eventually, these repetitions in relationships—at work, in friendships, and most importantly, in the family of origin—will replace an old feeling pattern with a new, more appropriate and useful one.

One of the main goals in managing oneself in relationships is to be able to be less reactive to the feeling states of those around one, unless of course one chooses to react. At the same time, communications are kept open and one remains accessible to others. When that is possible, the self-boundary stays intact.

The steps to be taken, then, in processing feelings can be summarized as:

- **Observe** the emotional state within the self and the system, as well as the trigger.
- **Think** about what has been observed and how to make sense of it.
- **Act.** No pattern ever changed simply by understanding it.

Dealing With Crises

The human phenomenon is serious and tragic, but at the very same time, there is a comical or humorous aspect to most serious situations.

Murray Bowen, 1971

Every relationship goes through periods of special stress. This occurs most notably when someone enters or leaves the relationship system of which the primary relationship is a part. Examples of this type of stress are marriage, birth of a child, death in the family, or divorce. These are referred to as "nodal events." At these times, anxiety in the system goes up. Other types of stress, however, can certainly affect relationships intensely enough to qualify as a crisis.

A crisis has been defined as a period of rapid change, a turning point, in which individual functioning is sometimes permanently altered, either toward a higher or a lower level. Clinical evidence indicates that relationships also can go on to higher or lower levels of functioning for very long times at the time of a crisis.

Bowen wrote about events that disturb family systems in the following way: *"The equilibrium of the unit is disturbed by either the addition of a new member or the loss of a member. The intensity of the emotional reaction is governed by the functioning level of emotional integration in the family at the time or by the functional importance of the one who is added to the family or lost to the family. For instance, the birth of a child can disturb the emotional balance until family members can realign themselves around the child. A grandparent who comes for a visit may shift family emotional forces briefly, but a grandparent who comes to live in a home can change the family emotional balance for a long period. Losses that can disturb the family equilibrium are physical losses, such as a child who goes away to college or an adult child who marries and leaves the home. There are functional losses, such as a key family member who becomes incapacitated with a long-term illness or injury that prevents his doing the work on which the family depends. There are emotional losses, such as the absence of a light-hearted person who can lighten the mood in a family. A group that changes from light-hearted laughter to seriousness becomes a different kind of organism. The length of time required for the family to establish a new emotional equilibrium depends on the emotional integration in the family and the intensity of the disturbance. . . . An attempt to get the family to express feelings at the moment of change does not necessarily increase the level of emotional integration."*

The "emotional shock wave" phenomenon was described by Bowen as an event that can have effects on a family system for an extended time. *"It occurs most often after the death of a significant family member, but it can be almost as severe after a threatened death. . . . A grandmother in her early sixties . . . had a radical mastectomy for cancer. Within the following two years, there was a chain of serious reactions in her children and their families. One son began drinking for the first time in his life, the wife of another son had a serious depression, a daughter's husband failed in business, and another daughter's children became involved in automobile accidents and delinquency. Some symptoms were continuing five years later when the grandmother's cancer was pronounced cured."*

When anxiety intensifies in an emotional system, it affects the thinking and behavior of the individuals who are part of the system, and their adaptability. Relationship patterns, if present, will tend to become more intense and automatic. Thinking is more difficult at times of increased anxiety, so people may do or say things they do not stand by in the longer term. Flexibility, one's ability to adapt to the changing circumstances, is reduced because of the increased anxiety. A greater-than-usual effort will be needed to manage one's emotions individually and in relationships.

During periods of unusual stress, or at any time of increased anxiety, standard "stress reduction" techniques, such as greater than usual amounts of physical and mental relaxation, are useful. Physically relaxed muscles mitigate anxiety and promote clear-headedness. Anxiety may be greatly reduced by physical exercise and playful activities. This is true whether the activity is done alone or with others. At a time of crisis, there never seem to be enough hours in the day, so these activities should be specially planned.

Relaxation and recreation, important as they are, must be balanced with finding ways of staying appropriately active in the crisis. Remaining in calm contact with all meaningful relationships in a system, as the crisis unfolds, is an active process. Quiet observation, the first step in understanding an anxious system, will have a calming effect. It makes thoughtful resolution of the crisis possible.

Nothing will ever be resolved, however, unless some action is taken. Thinking is absolutely essential, but so is action, based on the thinking. Action based only on emotion, on the other hand, usually turns out to be worse than no action at all.

During times of crisis, the constant, conscious effort to process one's own feelings will result in big payoffs in relationships. This means putting a stop to needless, thoughtless dumping of feelings into the relationship in favor of habitually taking responsibility for the processing of one's own feelings and reactions. This does not mean that other people cannot be a wonderful presence during a crisis or that some feeling processing cannot be done in relationships to the advantage of both people. Rather, it is a plea for a more judicious use of relationships in this way. After all, a significant other cannot really deal with one's feelings for one. Processing feelings, in the final analysis, must be done by the self. Taking responsibility for one's feelings means learning greater and greater facility at processing those feelings. Out of this process comes the calm necessary to think one's way through a crisis.

So, in a period of rapid change, individual and relationship functioning is changed toward a higher or a lower level, permanently. How one handles one's emotional self during a crisis—whether one is able to observe emotional process in the system, use that information, and think about various options—can have profound effects on decision making, relationships, and whether the event can be used to push the self up to a higher level of differentiation.

TEN MISCONCEPTIONS THAT CAN DEFEAT A RELATIONSHIP AND TEN WAYS TO PROMOTE SUCCESS

> I did not agree with the numerous misinterpretations of theory about the human family, but I am also never in favor of telling others what they should believe.
>
> **Murray Bowen, 1988**

Most people bring a few misconceptions into their relationships. Here are some common ones.

1. "The other person will make me happy."

Happiness (and the pursuit of it) is an individual matter. Another person may enhance or detract from one's happiness, but the primary responsibility for happiness or lack of it remains with the self.

2. "I can change the other," (or an attempt to do it that may sound like, "If you cared about me you'd . . .").

Both are serious boundary intrusions that set one up for disappointment. Most relationships cannot bear that kind of load. Those can be hard beliefs to give up, but the sooner it is done, the better the relationship will fare. As with happiness, change is accomplished only by and for each individual.

3. "A differentiated person must be cold and unfeeling."

When people have spent years believing that spontaneous expression and processing of all feeling states in relationships represents a high level of functioning, they may hear choosing between thinking and feeling systems as intellectually defending against feelings. However, even at the highest levels of differentiation, the choice can be made to go with the feeling system. A logical intellectual process, one relatively free of anxiety, is quite different from the illogical, inconsistent, intellectualized verbalizations of a person whose thinking system, fused to the emotional system, is awash with anxiety.

4. "It is my right to respond from my emotions to my partner's anxiety."

The excuse given usually is, "It is too hard not to," followed by "Why should I do all the work?" Responding to anxiety with anxiety leads to escalation, intensification, and instability. Trying instead to see the other's anxiety states and whatever he or she does or says during them as the other person's emotional "trash" may be more useful. Most useful is doing mentally what one does with trash—throwing it out!

5. "This relationship will never get any better."

If one truly believes that, it probably won't. But how can one tell? Since any relationship can function at a better level if even one person in it changes, either one has the power to change things unilaterally at any time.

6. "I've changed myself all I can and things aren't any better."

To be alive is to change, so it probably is not true that one has changed all one can—unless one is dead. Even so, two people never change at the same time. If one partner has truly raised the level of differentiation, that one will have more patience. Giving the relationship time to adjust to the changes in level of maturity, and giving a partner time to come up to a new level of functioning, can make a big difference.

7. Whenever one "needs" to talk it out or get feelings out, the other must agree to listen.

The belief that talking about feelings is the only way to feel better or believing that relationships exist for the purpose of processing feelings is a common misconception. Although communicating must be a high priority for any well-functioning relationship, this attitude belies a lack of respect for boundaries. The other has a right not to communicate at any given time, just as one has the right to ask.

There are many ways to change feeling states. The nature of feelings is that they come and go. Talking them out is only one of many ways to affect these states, and probably one that, if used exclusively, no relationship can tolerate. If one can take primary responsibility for processing feelings and be selective about which feelings to bring into the relationship, the relationship will do better.

8. Excessive worry about the past—your own or the other person's—is often defeating to relationships.

The belief that expressions of blame towards one's family of origin somehow help one advance is especially prevalent. However, if the past can be relegated to the past, most relationships (especially those in the original family) will do better.

9. "If you don't love me like my mother did, you don't love me."

Only one person will ever love one like one's mother.

10. "I can cut off from my extended family and still have good relationships."

It may be possible for some people, but a family of origin cutoff would, theoretically, stack the odds heavily against good nuclear family or other present relationships.

Ten Ways to Promote Relationship Success

> The "I position" defines principle and action in terms of, "This is what
> I think or believe" and "This is what I will do or will not do," without
> impinging one's own values or beliefs on others.
>
> Murray Bowen, 1972

Here are some typical statements made by people who have used
Bowen family systems theory ideals successfully in their primary
relationships.

1. "Working toward my own emotional calm and intellectual
objectivity enables me to think more clearly and thus speak and act
more constructively as well as providing a tangible contribution to the
emotional climate of relationships."

It is not necessary to be a victim of the emotional climate of others.
Playing one's full fifty percent in the relationship can make the climate
what one would like it to be.

2. "I am at my best in relationships when I can observe myself in a
relationship pattern and change my part in it without expectations of
the other."

Taking responsibility for the self is a full-time job for most people. It
is probably the biggest part of the work that must be done in
relationships.

3. "Staying in contact, maintaining one-to-one relationships with the
individuals in my systems is important for me—it provides a sense of
groundedness I have in no other way."

People caught in the cutoff pattern of their system try to carry it on
one more generation. Invariably they find that this style of relationship functioning works no better for them than it did for previous

generations. A cutoff system is an intense system. Intensity over time will translate into relationship difficulties.

4. "It doesn't matter who makes the contact (is the initiator) or if one person makes more than his or her share of contacts. What matters is that they are made."

To be present and accounted for, especially in a relatively cutoff system, may mean that one sometimes gets the feeling that one is doing more than one's share of the work. However, people who function at higher levels, while they are calmer, are also active systems forces. So, if one is doing more than others in a system, it should be seen as a tribute to the level one has reached.

5. "If I can remember to look for the anxiety behind the boundary intrusions of the others, I can be less reactive, managing myself better around them. They are usually not meant to be invasive."

Any communications made out of anxiety call for better-than-usual attempts to manage the emotional self. If the other person is seen as an anxious person, rather than as pompous, overbearing, arrogant, or malicious, he or she can be dealt with differently.

6. "It is not necessary for me to take on the emotions of the people I am around. I have a choice."

As one pushes up to higher levels of differentiation, not only is there more choice between thinking and automatic reactions, but self-boundaries are also more intact. The emotional reactions of others can thus remain theirs. They don't have to become the other's.

7. "I do not need to be loved, liked, approved of, accepted, or nurtured by the environment."

At lower levels of differentiation, approval of others can be an orienting factor, but as one moves up in level of functioning, it becomes more important to be clear about one's own inner guidance. Approval and acceptance are taken into consideration, but they are not the primary motivators.

8. "Keeping my focus primarily on the self (thinking of myself and my own life course at least 51 percent of the time), I can usually find a way to manage my emotional self in and out of relationships just a little better without being critical of myself or blaming anyone else."

Focusing that amazing brain on the functioning of the self, especially the emotional self, is itself a high-level function that unusually successful people are very good at. Everyone can get better at it with practice.

9. "Important relationship decisions, if made calmly and thoughtfully, usually stand the test of time better than those that I impulsively give over entirely to feelings."

Clinical evidence shows that those who run their lives mostly in the world of feelings, making their decisions by how they feel, rather than by a careful, objective, thought process, live in a world of chaotic relationships.

10. "I work toward needing less togetherness. Acting on principle, I can choose companionship and cooperative group effort when that is the best use of my life energy."

At high levels of differentiation, people can be happy in or out of relationships. They are complete and do not need others to complete them. Perhaps partly because of the lack of need for them, their relationships function better. They have more energy to do what makes the best use of their talents and abilities as they contribute to the world.

LIVING OUT
THE THEORY

> The goal . . . is to rise up out of the emotional togetherness that binds
> us all.
>
> **Murray Bowen, 1976**

Whenever the principles of family systems theory are applied and
people begin to work on how they function emotionally, both as
individuals and in relationships, change is seen in more than one area
of their lives. As they work to raise their levels of emotional maturity,
they discover they are better able to manage themselves in many
situations. All their relationships begin to work better.

As relationships work better and as people are freed from former
levels of relationship distress, they often find they have more clarity
and direction for approaching goals. There is more energy available
for life in general.

Maintaining meaningful relationships with one's own family of
origin seems to spawn an emotional "groundedness," or calm, of its
own. This is true even when that family is involved in fairly turbulent
emotional patterns. The degree to which one can step back from
family emotions and still stay connected with individuals in the system will become an important determining factor in the individual's
success. The facts one learns about the self in that family and the use
one makes of these facts to further emotional maturity will influence
all relationships for the better.

Bowen stated, "That which is created in a relationship can be
changed in a relationship." There is no need to triangle, distance from
it, or cut it off. Any of the work one does on oneself in one relationship
will pay off in others. Family of origin work not only helps functioning in the family of origin but also in the nuclear family, the

workplace, and in friendships. By the same token, if one undertakes to do a little better in workplace relationships, one soon finds that work there has also paid off in better family relationships. Life is learning, and learning done in one relationship can be applied to others.

Friendships

> The theory states that the triangle, a three-person emotional configu-
> ration, is the molecule, or the basic building block of any emotional
> system, whether it is in the family or any other group. The triangle is
> the smallest stable relationship system.
>
> **Murray Bowen, 1976**

Friendship may be the ideal paradigm for all relationships. Many problems commonplace in more intense relationships happen less frequently or not at all in friendships. If all relationships could be managed more like friendships, much difficulty in relationships could be avoided. Why is it that relationships between friends follow a smoother course than relationships between parents and children, employers and employees, and even lovers?

One possible explanation might be that in a friendship a sense of play is preserved, affording relaxation and lowering the emotional intensity and subsequent anxiety present in the relationship. When anxiety is lower, each person can maintain equality, openness, and separate self boundaries more easily. Thus, if one could think of children, spouses, or parents as our friends, what differences would be found in those relationships? What adjustments need to be made to move toward a paradigm of friendship in all relationships?

Friends are part of one's personal emotional system, a system other than family that broadens and deepens with the passage of years. One's system of friends will have its own emotional system characteristics that will tend to function better and more meaningfully over time if one pursues the work of differentiating a self on an ongoing basis.

In extraordinary relationships between friends, openness and availability do not migrate toward individuality-stifling togetherness. Ideally, friends treat each other as equals. Although friendship systems are often referred to as "support" systems, the simple term "friendship system" may be just as useful, since the term "support" conjures a borrowing and lending of self. That is, if one is thinking of the self as needing support, one is placing oneself in an underfunctioning posture.

Friendships will last only when the friends are at the same level of differentiation. In time, since friendships become emotionally significant relationships, all of the concepts that apply to emotionally significant relationships come into play in significant friendships. It is possible for the same patterns to occur, depending on the levels of differentiation of the partners, their family patterns, and their sibling positions. The same principles can be used to think one's way out of and to change patterns that occur in friendships.

As one becomes more emotionally mature, one becomes more attractive to others, gains more respect, and thus may have more friends. Also, as the level of differentiation is raised, the friends tend to be at a higher level also. Conversely, if the level of differentiation changes, even a little, some friendships may be lost because of the disparity that develops.

The research done by Dr. Walter Toman on sibling position (see Appendix III) is extremely valuable in explaining and predicting friendship preferences. As one goes to higher levels of differentiation, sibling position is less of a determinant and friendships may be more easily sustained with people from any sibling position.

Although people who are cut off from their families often can make significant gains working on differentiation of self through a friendship system, they will, in general, be much more successful if they work instead on the cutoffs that exist in their family of origin. However, if most or all of those family members are no longer living, it is possible to have some success in raising one's level of differentiation by working on it in a friendship system.

Love Relationships

> In broad terms, a person-to-person relationship is one in which two people can relate personally to each other about each other, without talking about others (triangling) and without talking about impersonal things . . . . In its ultimate sense, no one can ever know what a person-to-person relationship is, since the quality of any relationship can always be improved. On a more practical level, a person-to-person relationship is between two fairly well-differentiated people who can communicate directly, with mature respect for each other, without the complications between people who are less mature. The effort to work toward person-to-person relationships improves the relationship system in the family, and it is a valuable exercise in knowing self.
>
> **Murray Bowen, 1974.**

How is it possible to think most of the way through a book about relationships and rarely use the word "love"? Love is an interesting word. People think they know what they mean by it, but the problem comes in defining love and assuming everyone is using the same definition. It is probably one of the most ambiguous words in our language because of its emotional loading with old patterns that each person specifically attributes to it. In the consulting room, people express their frustration with trying to know what love is more than any other word.

Another problem with using the word "love" when attempting to be as specific and thoughtful as possible about relationships is its emotional charging value. To the extent that emotionally charged language is used in thinking, the thinking will be emotionally based, rather than rational and logical, so the outcome of the thinking is less dependable. Love is used as a reason to stay together, and lack of love as a reason to terminate a relationship. This line of thinking is indulged in most often by people who are living their lives based more on emotions than on thinking or inner guidance by principle.

Bowen theory, in order to bring the study of human behavior into the realm of science, stays with objective, observable facts. Love, a subjective concept, is difficult, if not impossible, to bring into that realm. The concept of "love", therefore, which generates more heat than light, was left out of the theory for some good reasons.

Emotions are, of course, prominent in mating. How could there be mating without them? It is the feeling side of the mating process that is rhapsodized, sonnetized, and lyricized. Love feels so good. But often an intense "loving" relationship can bring on a veritable jungle of precarious feeling states. At these times, a thoughtful substantial guide through the jungle is a welcome addition to the lyrics and the sonnets. Theory has been such a guide for many.

In order for relationships to get out of the intense roller-coaster of ups and downs so often reported, thought as well as feelings will have to be brought into play. If intense attractions could stop short of sexuality and revel in the delights of a "separate, equal, and open" friendship for a protracted period, is it possible that those intense relationships would have more chance for long-term success? Under those conditions, people would have more chance to explore guiding principles in a thoughtful way, learn whether it is possible to think independently in the company of the other, and see if a long-term friendship, upon which all solid relationships must be based, is possible. It would be possible to see if the emotional system about to be developed would be to the mutual advantage of the selves involved, for further building of self.

Couples often believe their problem is a sexual one. Sex therapists, however, find that by far the largest percentage of problems presented to them are relationship problems. That is, if the relationship were on a more even keel, the sexual problems would disappear. Family therapists often make the same discovery. As people learn a new way of relating that makes it possible to think calmly together, with each managing his or her own emotional self better over time, relationship problems become solvable, including sexual ones.

Does that mean ideal relationships are not intense and intensely loving? Probably not, but it may mean the intensity, when it is there, will be chosen and even to some degree controlled, rather than allowed to victimize and dominate the relationship. Ideally, if the more emotionally neutral friendship stage of relationships could last much longer than it often does, couples could build a more substantial relationship base upon which to ground their intensities. If later they decided to be intensely feeling and sexual with each other, the feelings and sex would be an expression of a solid relationship, one built over time.

At high levels of differentiation, it is hypothesized that a love relationship would develop slowly and calmly, from mutual attraction, into an active, working, and long-lasting friendship. The friendship could sustain itself even if the intense emotional part of the relationship turned out not to be a lasting one. At high levels, emotions would be chosen more often rather than dictating the situation. Spontaneity could be allowed; there would simply be more choice. Since boundaries are relatively separate, the relationship would not be subject to emotional piquing, escalation, and trading of self. Equality would not be an issue—it would simply be assumed and present in all the actions and communications. Openness would be a given and the primary tool for problem-solving if problems arose.

It has been said many times that the ability to love is based on one's ability to love oneself. What is the meaning of self-love? People often have a problem thinking of how to love the self. Yet they can readily fantasize love with another person. It may be that love of the self involves an ongoing relationship with the self that is all one would like relationships with others to be. This involves selecting some carefully considered guiding principles about how one thinks about oneself and making them a part of the basic self.

Often, depressed or suicidal people think very unfair, punitive, and even violent thoughts toward themselves. When the line of thought is examined, they admit that if it were directed toward anyone else, they would consider this line of thinking inappropriate, illogical, and unproductive. They have not admitted themselves into the human race. If they could think about themselves with the same principles they use toward others, the problem would be solved. They would be on the road to a principled way of being with the self.

What then is love? When all is said and done what does it mean to love someone? The view of love derived from family systems theory is entirely different from any other view. Perhaps it is a refreshing view that stands in contrast to the view represented on television, in movies and in the culture in general. The most loving that one can be may at the same time be the most difficult way of being, requiring the best that is in one. A loving relationship requires effort to keep the big picture, the process, the system, and one's principles constantly in mind. It requires effort to keep one's boundaries well tended and intact. Equality and openness must be worked at. If one loves, one will be loved, but not all the time.

Perhaps the highest form of loving is, through all the emotional excitement of togetherness, simply to be able to maintain a separateness that focuses on being the best self one can be and defining that self, while remaining in calm, thoughtful, meaningful contact with the other, accepting the efforts of the other at being the best self he or she can be over time.

Relationships Between Parents and Children

> The child-focused energy is deeply imbedded, and it includes the full range of emotional involvements from the most positive to the most negative. The higher the anxiety in the parents, the more intense the process.
>
> Murray Bowen, 1975

Being a parent may be the most difficult, most anxiety producing, and most important role in life. But theory can provide important guidelines for the task. Because it is possible to push one's level of differentiation higher, it is possible, to some extent, to lessen the flow of undifferentiation into the next and future generations.

Having a relationship with each child is vitally important. Although this might seem basic, it is surprising how often parents have no real relationship with offspring, despite the fact that there may be plenty of interaction or focus. In large or very busy families, this seemingly obvious principle must be given priority, and time for each child must be planned. Clinicians see significant problems of children or teenagers turn around rapidly when one or both parents find time for a personal relationship with them.

Like all relationships, the ideal parent-child relationship is characterized by equality, separateness, and openness. How can a relationship between an adult and a child or infant be a relationship of equals? While they are not equals in strengths and skills, a parent can relate to a child as an equal in potential and in basic humanness. The automatic "doing for" posture that disables the child by playing to his or her weaknesses will be lessened. A cooperative stance with the child will be the norm, instead of an overfunctioning or competitive one. This posture will be returned in kind by the child over time.

Mutual respect between parent and child is fostered when the separate boundaries of each self are observed. Intact boundaries mean less automatic reactivity. If one is anxious, the other can choose to stay calm. If anyone in a family is working on improving boundaries of the self and is respecting the boundaries of the others, the others in the family will gradually, and sometimes rather quickly, do likewise. Thus, it becomes less likely that anxiety will come to rest in or get focused on any one member of the family. Just having the notion of boundaries clearly in mind makes it more likely that they will be worked on and respected.

Open communication with the next generation, when guided by Bowen theory, differs from what is usually advocated and practiced. The preoccupation with feelings often promoted is absent. Although an understanding of others' feelings grows out of a well-developed understanding of one's own emotional systems (both internal and external to the self), it can be safely assumed that each individual is capable and adequate to the task of processing his or her own feelings. If one is respecting boundaries in interactions, it is not necessary to always check on the other's feelings—there will be fewer intrusions and thus less anxiety. Also, one is perfectly free, in such a system, to define feelings to the other, if that is important, knowing that the other will not become overly reactive as a result. So, although feelings are recognized, it is not necessary for parents and children to spend as much time outwardly processing the feelings in their relationship system.

Openness in verbal communication with children implies a willingness to define one's thinking to them. It should not be taken for granted that offspring know what one thinks. Often clinicians ask parents if they have ever told their children what they have just said to the clinician. Very often, the parents answer, "They know what I think!" But they may not. One often does not define oneself calmly and clearly to youngsters in a way that enables them to hear.

Speaking is done for the self and the self only. It is perfectly possible for a parent to clearly define his or her own principles to the next generation—principles that have been carefully fashioned out of experience and thought—without telling them what to do. That is, a parent can define the self, while still respecting boundaries and the right of people to differ and be different. Often, it seems parents are reticent to talk about what they really believe in or to say what they really think. But that is, after all, part of being a self, and it is very useful to children, even when they don't quite see it the way the parents do. With open communication, children will have the advantage of growing up around a self. Distance does not become a problem.

As growing children and teenagers become more articulate, it is of extreme importance that parents assume an interested listener role some of the time. Listening is a skill many parents, sadly, never learn. But how are children going to become skilled at defining their thoughts in words if no one ever listens to them?

Focusing on self a major portion of time and a well-functioning marital relationship preclude child focus. And, although anxiety will travel around triangles as long as humans live in families, if open one-to-one relationships are maintained, with each self making an effort to define self and no one else, there will be fewer casualties of the family emotional process. If a child in a family begins to draw a disproportionate amount of focus, it is safe to suppose anxiety that properly belongs between the spouses has not been dealt with between them. When the child focus is lessened, the marital problem emerges and can be dealt with.

If, instead of being resolved by the spouses, however, marital anxiety moves around the triangles of the family system, it may eventually center on one of the children. Being the center of an anxious focus guarantees a high degree of anxiety in that person, and eventually symptoms—physical, mental, emotional, or social—will appear. Symptoms of the focused child include underachievement at school, school phobias, depression, hyperactivity, psychosis, addictions, peer-relationship problems, rebelliousness, and many others.

If parents work on the relationship problem between them, the child or teenager will respond with a reduction or disappearance of symptoms. Freed of the anxiety that was stifling personal progress, the child is able to get on with the process of developing a self. Even when parents work very hard on their part of the problem, the symptoms of the focused child will sometimes reappear. This may be because the child focus is an old pattern that several members of the family have lived with over a significant period of time. Patterned behavior changes slowly. But each time the symptoms reappear, they are weaker and briefer. If the parents can stay on course, both with themselves and with each other, the problems of the child will eventually diminish significantly or disappear altogether.

The worried, anxious focus is replaced by the parents' confident interest in the child—an attitude that leaves the life problems of the child to the child to solve. Often, it is also an attitude the parents have had all along toward other children in the family who are doing better. When parents take seriously the idea of differentiating a self in all the emotional systems in which they are involved, clarifying boundaries, thinking, and moving on principle, everyone in the emotional system benefits, especially growing children.

After divorce, it is important for the two parents to get to emotional neutrality towards each other as soon as possible, bridging any cutoff that may have developed during the divorce process. It is surprising to see what has been done in some families in this regard. While new spouses in remarriage can sometimes pose an initial problem to the relating of two ex-spouses, the ex-spouses can have a continued relationship that the new spouses will, in time, accept. Children in a divorced family can be expected to do about as well with divorce as the parents themselves do. Even in a divorce, a child focus is not a good solution to problems created by family emotional process.

While the child-focus pattern is the most common in the parent-child relationship, it is possible for parents and their children to assume any of the relationship postures. They can be distant, not communicating, or even cut off at times. They can be conflictual—openly fighting with each other or grappling with conformity or rebellion issues. Either parent or child can be in the overfunctioning or underfunctioning position. And anxiety is always moving around the triangles of the family. Understanding the triangles better means dealing with them better.

Of all the legacies a parent can give children, by far the best is that of raising his or her own level of differentiation as high as possible in a generation. If that is the parental focus, the children will automatically function better.

Divorce

> The one who runs away . . . needs emotional closeness but is allergic to it . . . kidding himself that he is achieving "independence." . . . The more intense the cutoffs with his parents the more he is vulnerable to repeating the same pattern in future relationships . . . . He can have an intense relationship in a marriage, which he sees as ideal and permanent at the time, but the physical distance pattern is part of him. When tension mounts in the marriage, he will use the same pattern of running away.
>
> **Murray Bowen, 1974**

When seemingly moribund families begin to work with principles of Bowen family systems theory, divorce often becomes unnecessary. Unless one works at moving one's functioning to a higher level, divorce will probably solve nothing. The same immaturity and patterned functioning will find ways of working themselves out in a succession of relationships no better or worse than the old ones.

If divorce occurs, however, theory can show the way while moving through it. Keeping one's own anxiety processed will aid clear thinking, essential in any crisis. Being aware of the rapidity with which triangles form among families, partners, children, the legal profession, and the courts is basic to managing the emotional self through such a time. Seeing the big picture by trying for systems thinking can resolve many dilemmas. Watching for emotional process can help to keep one more out of it and on course.

After a divorce, it is often useful to reestablish emotionally neutral contact with the divorced partner as soon as possible if it has been lost during the legal process. If this can be done and continued over time, the mourning and devastating depression that often follow divorce is often ameliorated. That depression may be intensified, however, by the effects of cutoff.

Avoidance of cutoff is especially important if there are children. If the two parents can preserve an emotionally calm relationship, the children will benefit greatly. This is in contrast to those relationships where chronic conflict, competition, or cutoff is the rule.

Mrs. A remained cut off from her ex-husband three years after her divorce, except for necessary communications about their four-year-old daughter's visitation schedule. Mrs. A was depressed. Her daughter was manipulative and was noted by her teacher to have problems lying and hitting other children. Then Mrs. A having learned some relationship principles, decided to try for a more open and cooperative relationship with her ex-husband. In the beginning of her effort, he was suspicious of the change in her attitude, but she persisted. Rather than automatically reacting negatively when he would ask for a change in visitation, she tried to accommodate whenever possible. If there was a problem with their daughter, rather than getting upset and keeping it to herself, she would, after getting as calm and thoughtful as she could about it, explain her thinking to her daughter's father, asking what he thought, using him as a resource.

Not only did the two divorced parents, in time, find that two heads could be more useful than one in thinking about a problem around their daughter's behavior, but in several months, Mrs. A was able to see that the relationship between herself and her ex-husband was on a much better level. As a result Mrs. A noted less depression in herself. She also noted that her relationship with her daughter worked much better; she could be more a parent, rather than fluctuating between boss and sibling. Her daughter's behavioral problems diminished.

Many families have attested to the emotional relief they experience when they get in contact with, and maintain relationships with, ex-spouses. Once the relationship is re-established after the usual cut-off represented by divorce, working toward separate boundaries, openness, and an equal stance become important here as in other relationships. Children of divorce who are lucky enough to have one parent working in this way often show the positive effects.

The Single Life

> The degree of unresolved emotional attachment to parents is determined by the degree of unresolved emotional attachment each parent had in their own family of origin, the way their parents handled this in their marriage, the degree of anxiety during critical periods in life, and the way the parents handled this anxiety. The child is "programmed" into the emotional configuration very early in life, following which the amount of unresolved emotional attachment remains relatively fixed except for functional shifts in the parents . . . In broad terms, the amount of anxiety tends to parallel the degree of unresolved emotional attachment in the family.
>
> **Murray Bowen, 1974**

At high levels of differentiation people can be comfortable in or out of relationships.

There are very few people who do not have any relationships, even though they may be single. If they look around them, life is full of opportunity for relationships. Almost everyone has extended family relationships, friendships, and work relationships, all of which can benefit by work on the self in the relationship. If these relationships are taken as personal challenges, they can become fascinating projects in the differentiation of a self. Getting on with this work detracts from the discomfort of being without a primary relationship.

Single persons have a wonderful opportunity to develop that most paramount of all relationships, the relationship with the self. Being single enables one to work on furthering one's individuality without the distraction and risk of fusion into an intense relationship. Navigating a single lifestyle from principles derived from the concept of differentiation of self makes for a very different life course than what is often seen.

Just as married people may have to work to keep their individuality focused amid the togetherness in their lives, single people must sometimes work to provide enough relationships to test out their individuality. For it is only in relationship to one's emotional system that one can differentiate a self.

Friendship systems become extremely important to single people. A friendship system provides some of the emotional groundedness that living in a nuclear family does and may, for single people, become more intense because of the lack of a nuclear family. In that case, all the relationship principles become especially important as guidelines.

Professional Relationships

> Terms such as "people," "person," and "family member" replaced the term "patient." Diagnoses were avoided, even in the therapist's private thinking. It has been more difficult to replace the concepts of "treatment," "therapy," and "therapist" and to modify the omnipotent position of the therapist to the patient. . . . Terms such as "supervisor," "teacher," and "coach" are probably best in conveying the connotation of an active expert coaching both individual players and the team to the best of their abilities.
>
> **Murray Bowen, 1975**

The professional/client relationship is at risk for all the relationship patterns but, by its very nature, is especially vulnerable to the overfunctioning/underfunctioning reciprocity pattern: One person is asking for help for a problem; the other is trained to give help.

What is overfunctioning in the professional situation? How can the professional relate to people who have problems without overfunctioning?

A study of 15 people addicted to prescription medications taught the author much about the professional relationship. The addicted people initially appeared to be helpless, hopeless, and unable to cope without their medication. They were in a posture of underfunctioning in their primary relationships and had duplicated the pattern with their primary physicians, who, in an effort to be helpful, had prescribed the medicine. It was found that this relationship posture was a repetition of an early life relationship posture.

Underfunctioning behaviors observed included whining, weeping, presentation of self as inadequate, hopeless, or in a corner with no options. Some of the overfunctioning behaviors of the physician or consultant were advising, overteaching (knowing what someone else should think), preaching (knowing what someone else should do), and overhelping (to the point of overprescribing).

The ideal professional/client relationship can be described in the same way as any ideal relationship: separate, equal, and open. If the professional is clear about the emotional boundaries of self, and practiced at living within them, emotional neutrality will be easier. While the client may be looking intensely for a fused relationship in which he or she is in the underfunctioning position, the professional who knows about relationship patterns can resist them.

The professional can also know about his or her own tendencies to overfunction. This may, in fact, have been a motivation in the choice of profession. Knowing about relationship process tendencies in oneself can be an advantage in learning to deal with them.

Ideally, a professional can relate to and encourage a person's ability, focusing on what is right with people: their strengths and those of their families. The addicted patients' presentation as hopeless, helpless, and weak was of a curiously demanding nature that actually belied a tremendous strength. When it is possible for the professional to see and relate to the strength and ability of the person, the professional/client relationship is on the way toward becoming a relationship of equals.

How can a professional, an expert, relate to a client as an equal? Actually, the possession of skills, training, or knowledge need not create an unequal situation in a human encounter any more than the wearing of different clothes would. A basic equality as humans can be recognized, acknowledged, and assumed by the professional.

Openness in the professional relationship is necessary for its optimal functioning, whether it be in the arena of medicine, nursing, therapy, or the law. The more anxious the client, the more difficult it is to listen, but it remains one of the most important skills any professional can develop. Professional responses are made from thinking rather than from emotion, if the relationship is to be productive in the tasks assigned to it. Openness is not served by the professional who uses jargon—words specific to his or her discipline—that the client does not understand. As noted before, effective communication will exist only to the degree that relationship patterns do not exist.

If the overfunctioning pitfall is avoided, other patterns can threaten the process, unless one is working on one's own differentiation of self. Distance might show up in the form of the professional becoming underactive in the work, not answering phone calls, or being vague. Conflict with a client can turn up in a style of communicating ideas or in frequent disagreements. Triangling can be swift and automatic when other family members or agencies are drawn in. Cutoff can occur when the content or the process of the professional work is not handled expertly.

As in any other relationship, resorting to one relationship pattern in order to be rid of another solves nothing, although it is a fairly universal and automatic human response. However, when principles of relationship theory are understood and used, especially when the professional is working on attainment of a higher level of differentiation of self, management of the emotional self of the professional comes into clearer focus.

Workplace Relationships

> With an impersonal theory, it simply meant the focus was always on self instead of the other. This was used constantly in all administrative systems. When there was conflict or disharmony in the work system at Georgetown, it simply meant that self had played a part, and if self modified his part, the others would automatically change their part. The model has worked well through the years.
>
> **Murray Bowen, 1988**

The primary emphasis in the workplace is on competency for completing the work. However, difficulty in the relationship system of the workplace often means that personal competency and efficiency suffer, interfering with production. Poorly functioning interpersonal relationships at work interfere with work output and perhaps cause more stress than any other single factor.

The principles regarding relationships apply in the workplace as they do to any other relationship system. When people spend a significant portion of time together, as they certainly do during a work week, they build up an emotional relationship system very similar to that of a family. Emotions pass from one person to another and triangles form along with the other relationship patterns seen in a family system.

The better the quality of the relationships in the workplace, the better the quality and the quantity of the work itself. Work systems themselves operate at different levels of differentiation, depending on the maturity levels of their leaders and also on the level of each individual in the system. The higher the level of differentiation of the individuals of the work system, the more efficiently it will run and the more productive it will be.

Relationship problems between leaders in the workplace may, and often do, filter down through the system by means of triangles, finding expression several levels down in the system in conflict, distance, or other patterned postures between individual workers. However, if there is a relationship difficulty at the top of the system, between the leaders, repeated firings (which may become the order of the day in such a system) will be of no use. The only real answer to this problem is for the leaders to improve their relationships with each other. When this happens, the system will run more smoothly.

Theory points the way for management just as surely as for everyone else in the workplace. Managers, because of their leadership positions, have more influence on the system. If they keep in mind principles of differentiation, think systems, and work toward separate boundaries, equality, and openness, the entire workplace system will benefit.

After competence (for which there is no substitute), relationships at work are the greatest single determinant of career success. Family systems principles are of great usefulness as guidelines for workplace relationships. Management of the self toward higher levels of functioning and working for emotional calm are especially useful at work. Ability to stay emotionally calm in the workplace is valued because when one is calm, the cerebral or thinking brain is not overburdened by anxiety generated in the emotional brain. Thus one is free to do better thinking—thinking about self-management as well as about the work itself. In other words, the ability to keep oneself emotionally calm frees one to do better work.

Emotionalism at work, far from solving anything, disrupts and interferes with getting the work done and can block career progress. The ability to choose emotional calm is essential to functioning well in any work place.

In the recent past, some workplace consultants, focusing the organization on the group processing of feelings, have led work groups into emotional chaos, with everyone thinking this kind of morass was somehow necessary or inevitable in order to straighten out relationship problems. Not only is this not necessary, it is counterproductive.

Staying in contact with each person in the workplace system using principles of good communications offers obvious benefits. Though relationship patterns will develop simply because they are so automatic to human behavior, they can be seen more objectively by one who is aware of them. This kind of objectivity can lead to better functioning in the triangles of the workplace. Better functioning in relationships often means that one comes to be seen as a valued individual in the work "family." Communications principles based on knowledge of the relationship patterns become as applicable in the workplace as they are in any other relationship system.

Since people who spend a significant portion of time together eventually develop an emotional system similar to that of a nuclear family, it helps to know the sibling positions in their families of origin of the people in the work system. Knowledge of sibling positions alone will tell one much about the personality and ways of relating to each person one works with. (See Appendix III.) Sibling position will also reveal much about potential natural strengths of various people in the workplace. This knowledge will be useful in seeing each person more objectively. As that happens, one becomes less prone to take perceived problems personally.

It is also helpful to know the approximate dates that each person joined the system. Working out for oneself the longevity of each person in the system will give you an appreciation of the relationship history of the system as it existed before one joined it. This understanding of the established triangles of the emotional system of one's workplace becomes invaluable as one attempts to move smoothly and productively among them. Knowledge of the relationship history of the system greatly enhances the handling of one's emotional self in it.

Places of work, like families, also go through periods of unusual stress, which tend to cause relationship patterns and postures to be more in evidence than usual. Periods of unusual stress might include a transitional time around changing of leaders, a period of economic change, or a company reorganization. At these times, it is more difficult for each individual to stay on course in the organization; that is, it becomes harder to stay out of triangles or out of polarized positions with or against factions that develop. But a goal during a period of intense anxiety remains to retain competent output by working for emotional calm and by staying in emotionally neutral contact with everyone in the system, regardless of their positions or factions.

If one stays on course, guided by inner principle, it is a differentiating position in the system. Added respect, promotions, and other rewards have been noted by some people who stayed with this kind of work for a significant period of time.

The efforts one makes with relationships at work have a beneficial effect on the rest of one's relationships. In the same way, increasing one's functioning in the family has a beneficial effect on one's functioning at work.

Societal Process and International Relationships

> The human is a narcissistic creature who lives in the present and who
> is more interested in his own square inch of real estate, and more
> devoted to fighting for his rights than in the multigenerational meaning
> of life itself. As the human throng becomes more violent and unruly,
> there will be those who survive it all. . . . I think the differentiation of
> self may well be one concept that lives into the future . . . . The future
> is limitless.
>
> **Murray Bowen, 1988**

The last concept to be added to Bowen theory is that of societal regression. It notes that, periodically, as anxiety begins to run higher in society, regressed behavior can be noted on a massive scale. A hallmark of such an anxious period is the unwillingness of families or other institutions of society (such as the court system) to take responsibility when behavior breaks down.

It is theorized that periods of regression alternate with periods of progression, in which responsibility in individuals, families, and societal institutions can be seen more readily. The alternating cycle is often referred to as *societal process*. Periods of progression are presumed to occur at times of less anxiety in society.

Some triggers of societal anxiety at the present time might be overpopulation, lack of resources (perhaps the same problem), pollution, and the nuclear-weapons threat.

Dr. John B. Calhoun, working at the National Institutes of Health, found when a rat population was allowed to breed for several generations in confined quarters, the resulting overcrowding led to regressive behavior. Males abandoned their guarding-of nests behavior and mothers forgot how to make effective nests, leaving the young exposed and vulnerable. As the overcrowding progressed, females and males lost interest in one another. The females followed anything that moved, such as the experimenter himself, and males hung out in the periphery of the quarters, staring. Eventually procreation declined and the population decreased.

In a crisis in society, just as in a family, mounting anxiety moves intensely around triangles that become more evident than they were in calmer times. Polarized factions take the spotlight, thinking only of their emotionally based interpretations of the facts rather than trying to see the bigger picture or looking at the welfare of the whole of society.

It seems clear that a societal regression is currently taking place. The importance of a theory that can inform human leadership at this time is apparent.

In international relations, if leaders and countries can begin to make decisions that reflect an understanding of differentiation of self, acting responsibly from knowledge of facts rather than from the emotional process of society, it may be that *Homo sapiens* has a chance to survive.

If the world is ever to get from troubled and unpredictable international relations to international relationships that are durable and trustworthy, perhaps it will be necessary for a new theory to eventually inform the thinking and moving of the political and diplomatic leaders of the world.

Most often the primary problem in international relations is seen as a matter of conflict resolution. Many programs, conferences, grants, and organizations are designed with conflict resolution in mind. That is, no doubt, useful—as far as it goes. However, conflict, important as it is to understand, is only one of five relationship postures into which people, and perhaps countries, become locked. For conflict to be understood, it would seem that all the postures must be known and explored.

Negotiations experts have learned a great deal about how to manage the give-and-take of the negotiation process. Yet sometimes negotiations bog down when it comes to having a way to think theoretically about the relationship between the negotiating parties.

Workshops aimed at considering the usefulness of Bowen theory in the international relations arena have been informative. Often audiences are quicker to see the application of Bowen theory to international relations than families are to their private lives.

What would happen, for example, at the academic level, if those who now are involved in the problem of conflict resolution broadened their understanding of relationship patterns to include the other four patterns: distance, cutoff, over- and underfunctioning, and triangles? What part do the other patterns play in the kind of conflict that leads ultimately to war? And, short of war, how much human misery is bound up in these patterns? Perhaps all the patterns lead to a kind of desperation that makes war seem a favorable outcome.

If nations can be said to have postures one to the other, what would a distant posture between two nations look like? How about overfunctioning/underfunctioning? Triangling? And how does conflict look between nations when it becomes a pattern?

If the antidote to personal relationship patterning is moving on to a higher level of differentiation of self, can a whole nation do that? Is it possible that a nation can be guided more by carefully considered principles than by its automatic reactivity? How clear are the principles of a nation? How does a nation define its principles in the world? Is it possible that some nations of the world exhibit a higher level of differentiation than others?

If violence erupts in the world, how does a country respond if it is attempting to move according to principle? Does such a country have an obligation when human rights are violated? When is one moving according to principle and when are boundaries being violated? What is the difference between boundary violation and boundary setting?

How does Bowen theory inform national leadership? If a leader were highly differentiated and moving on principle, would the nation move with him or her?

Here is what Bowen wrote on the subject:

> In a small or large social system, the move toward individuality is initiated by a single, strong leader with the courage of his conviction who can assemble a team, and who has clearly defined principles on which he can base his decisions when the emotional opposition

becomes intense. The large social system goes through the same small steps with rebalancing the togetherness-individuality forces after each step. There is never a threat of too much individuality. The human need for togetherness prevents going beyond a critical point. A society with higher levels of individuality provides great growth for individuals in the group, it handles anxiety well, decisions are based on principle and are easy, and the group is attractive to new members. This was characteristic of the United States for most of its history. The founders of the nation were strong on principles that provided flexible guarantees for individual rights and were attractive to immigrants from everywhere. The breakdown in individuality starts when leaders become lax in maintaining principles. When the next anxiety episode occurs, the leaders are sufficiently unsure of principles to begin making decisions based on the anxiety of the moment and the togetherness forces again become dominant. . . .

. . . .If the most influential segment of society could work toward the differentiation of self, it would automatically spread through the less influential segments and really benefit the less fortunate segment and raise the functional level of all society. The powerful togetherness forces in society oppose any efforts at differentiation of self. The lower the level of differentiation, the harder it is to start a differentiating effort. The togetherness forces at the present are intense. However, any differentiation in any key person in society automatically rubs off on others. Anyone who moves in this direction benefits society.

Epilogue

The possibility of extraordinary relationship as seen through the lens of Bowen family systems theory demonstrates anew the paradoxical nature of human existence. If one wants to work on a relationship, one must work on oneself. If one wants to work on individuality, it is best done in relationship to others. In order to be less distant, one must develop better boundaries. A thoughtful book raises more questions than it answers, and it jumps unhesitatingly into the paradoxes.

Most of the concepts introduced in this book have been presented in their simplest forms. Thorough understanding of Bowen theory requires further study. A list of the best sources available is found in the Reading Notes section.

It's difficult, at this point, to find a consultant trained in Bowen family systems theory. The number of trained professionals is growing, however. Besides the training center in Washington, D.C., there are centers for training in Chicago, Vermont, Princeton, Kansas City, Pittsburgh, San Francisco, South Carolina, Florida, Minneapolis, and elsewhere. Some of these centers offer training courses for professionals and, often, community courses as well.

Professionals trained in Bowen theory refer to the consulting process as "coaching" because so little of the useful work of self-change actually occurs in the consulting room. It is done instead in the "field" of the family.

I believe the study of relationships is the most important of human endeavors at the present time. It looks very much as though if that study is not given high priority, *Homo sapiens* may find itself on the way to rapid extinction. Bowen theory is a useful way to approach inquiry into a science of relationships of all kinds, including the troubled moving, posturing, and positioning of nation toward nation in the family of humankind.

At his funeral on October 20, 1990, I was honored to be able to read parts of the following thoughts from Dr. Bowen's writings.

Man has overcome many of the forces that threatened his existence in former centuries. His life span has been increased by medical science, his technology has advanced rapidly, he has become increasingly more in control of his environment, which has been his adversary, and a higher percentage of the world's population has more economic security and creature comforts than at any time during man's history on earth . . . . By the late 1960s, there was a hypothesis that has not only held up for several years, but that has also been strengthened by new evidence and the work of others. The hypothesis postulates that man's increasing anxiety is a product of population explosion, the disappearance of new habitable land to colonize, the approaching depletion of raw materials necessary to sustain life, and growing awareness that "spaceship earth" cannot indefinitely support human life in the style to which man and his technology have become accustomed. Man is a territorial animal who reacts to being "hemmed in" with the same basic patterns as the lower forms of life. Man tells himself other reasons to explain his behavior while important life patterns are the same as for non-thinking animals. Man has always used "getting away from the crowd" as a way of allaying anxiety and stabilizing his adjustment. The thesis here is that man became increasingly aware that his world is limited in size through rapid communication and television, and rapid travel. When animals are confined to a limited space, their numbers are increasing, they test the limits of the compound, there is more mobility and moving around, and they finally come to live more in piles that spread evenly over existing space. Man has become more mobile the past twenty-five years, more people move more often, and a higher percentage of the population is coming to live in the large metropolitan centers.

Another theoretical notion is important to this background thinking; it is another predictable characteristic of man. With his logical thinking and knowledge, he could have known decades ago that he was on a collision course with his environment. His emotions, reactiveness, and its cause-and-effect thinking prevent him from really "knowing" what he could know . . . Science has enabled man to get beyond cause-and-effect thinking in many areas of life. He was first able to use systems in astronomy, far removed from him personally. Later he was able to "think systems" about the physical sciences, and later in the natural sciences. In the past decades, he has had some notion that systems thinking also applies to himself and his own emotional functioning, but in an emotional field, even the most disciplined systems thinker reverts to cause-and-effect thinking and to taking action based more on emotional reactiveness than objective thinking. This phenomenon plays an important part in man's decisions and actions about social problems.

Reading Notes

The format for these reading notes was inspired by that of "Biophilia" by Edward O. Wilson.

Part I.
A New Way of Thinking About Relationships
Chapter 1.—Dr. Bowen's Extraordinary Way of Thinking

Bowen quote from Bowen, M.: *Family Therapy in Clinical Practice,* New York, Jason Aronson, 1978, p. 393.

Dr. Bowen told his own story in one of his last major works, "An Odyssey Toward Science," the epilogue of *Family Evaluation* by Michael Kerr and Murray Bowen, New York, Norton and Co., 1988.

Chapter 2.—A Theory About Relationships

Bowen quote from "An Odyssey Toward Science," the epilogue of *Family Evaluation* by Michael Kerr and Murray Bowen, New York, Norton and Co., 1988.

The original written source for theoretical ideas is the collection of Dr. Bowen's major papers, *Family Therapy in Clinical Practice* by Murray Bowen, New York, Jason Aronson, 1978.

Theory is not learned best solely from the written word. Many of the ideas presented in this book came out of my course work at the Georgetown University Family Center with Dr. Bowen and faculty members Dr. Michael Kerr, Mrs. Kathleen Kerr, Dr. Roberta Holt, Dr. Daniel Papero, and others.

Information on training programs, as well as publications, audiotapes, and videotapes can be obtained by writing:

Georgetown Family Center
4400 MacArthur Blvd. N.W., Ste 102
Washington, DC 20007

Chapter 3.—Differentiation of Self

Bowen quote from Bowen, M.: *Family Therapy in Clinical Practice,* New York, Jason Aronson, 1978, p. 424.

Bowen quote from "An Odyssey Toward Science," the epilogue of *Family Evaluation* by Michael Kerr and Murray Bowen, New York, Norton and Co., 1988, p. 168.

Dr. Michael Kerr's lectures on the work of Leo Buss on the individuation of cells has clarified the pervasiveness of the forces of individuality and togetherness at many levels.

Priscilla Friesen Felton's lectures emphasizing the phenomenon of marriage following family death were important.

Goodall's observations are documented in her several books. One concise summary of her work is found in *Understanding Chimpanzees,* edited by P. Heltne and L. Marquardt, Harvard University Press in cooperation with the Chicago Academy of Sciences, Cambridge, Mass., and London, England, 1989. See p. 27 for the Flo and Flint story.

The nature of differentiation of self was clarified by the thinking of Kathleen Kerr concerning the basic self as the inner guidance system, and self boundaries as being relatively more or less permeable, in several presentations summarized in the *Family Center Report,* summer, 1988.

Clarification on the nature of the inner guidance systems was provided in Daniel Papero's academic lectures at the Georgetown Family Center as well as in "Family Systems and Marriage," in progress for *Clinical Handbook of Marital Therapy,* Guilford Press.

Chapter 4.—Thinking Systems, Watching Process

Bowen quote from Bowen M.: *Family Therapy in Clinical Practice,* New York, Jason Aronson, 1978, p. 418-420. Quote on triangles pp. 478-479.

MacLean, Paul: *A Triune Concept of Brain and Behavior,* Toronto and Buffalo, University of Toronto Press, 1973.

Goodall, J., *Through a Window, My Thirty Years With the Chimpanzees of Gombe,* Boston, Houghton Mifflin, 1990.

deWaal, F., *Chimpanzee Politics,* Baltimore, Johns Hopkins University Press, 1982, 1989.

Chapter 5.—Relationship Patterns and Postures

Bowen quote from Bowen, M.: *Family Therapy in Clinical Practice,* New York, Jason Aronson, 1978, p. 476.

MacLean, Paul, quote from *A Triune Concept of the Brain and Behavior,* Toronto and Buffalo, University of Toronto Press, 1973.

Most of these concepts are to be found in Dr. Murray Bowen's *Family Therapy in Clinical Practice,* New York, Jason Aronson, 1978.

Chapter 6.—Emotions in Relationships

Bowen quote from "An Odyssey Toward Science," the epilogue of *Family Evaluation* by Michael Kerr and Murray Bowen, New York, Norton and Co., 1988, p. 360.

Dr. Paul MacLean's work on the triune brain informs descriptions of the survival aspects of the emotional system. See *A Triune Concept of the Brain and Behavior,* Toronto and Buffalo, University of Toronto Press, 1973.

Chapter 7.—Conflict

Bowen quote from Bowen, M.: *Family Therapy in Clinical Practice,* New York, Jason Aronson, 1978, pp. 377-378.

Chapter 8.—Distance

Kathleen Kerr's simple statement in lectures, 1986, about making contact, "Humans know when they have, and when they haven't," was the best antidote for the distance posture I have heard.

Frans deWaal's descriptions of animal behavior are found in deWaal, F.: *Chimpanzee Politics,* Baltimore, Johns Hopkins University Press, 1982, and in deWaal, F.: *Peacemaking Among Primates,* Cambridge, Harvard University Press, 1989.

Chapter 9.—Cutoff
Bowen quote from Bowen, M.: *Family Therapy in Clinical Practice,* Jason Aronson, New York, 1978, p. 536.

The story of the generic opera plot was given on the radio several years ago by an unknown narrator.

Chapter 10.—Overfunctioning/Underfunctioning Reciprocity
Bowen quote from Bowen M.: *Family Therapy in Clinical Practice,* Jason Aronson, New York, 1978, p. 378.

Chapter 11.—Triangles
Bowen quote from Bowen, M.: *Family Therapy in Clinical Practice,* Jason Aronson, New York, 1978, p. 478.

Chapter 12.—Repetitions
Freud, S.: "The Dynamics of the Transference," in *Sigmund Freud, Collected Papers,* Vol. 2, Basic Books, New York, 1959.

On scientific theories, the old and the new: Motz, L., and Weaver, H.H.: *The Concepts of Science From Newton to Einstein,* Plenum Press, New York, 1988.

My thinking toward a Bowen family systems view of this subject was facilitated by the opportunity to give several presentations on the subject in courses at the Georgetown University Family Center.

Chapter 13.—Family Constellation and Sibling Position
This section was abstracted from *Family Constellation* by Walter Toman, 3rd edition, New York, Springer Publishing Co., 1976.

Chapter 14.—When Relationships Go Off Course
Bowen quote from Bowen, M.: *Family Therapy in Clinical Practice,* Jason Aronson, New York, 1978.

Part II.
Portrait of an Extraordinary Relationship

Bowen quote from Bowen, M.: *Family Therapy in Clinical Practice,* Jason Aronson, New York, 1978, p. 537.

My thinking about the characteristics of an ideal relationship was catalyzed by a diagram drawn by Dr. Roberta Holt during clinical supervision in my course work.

Chapter 15.—The Ideal: Separate, Equal, and Open

Bowen quote from Bowen, M.: *Family Therapy in Clinical Practice,* Jason Aronson, New York, 1978, pp. 364, 370, 473, 537.

The section on open communication in relationships was taken from a paper presented by the author at the Georgetown University Family Center's Annual Symposium, "What is Communication?" 1986.

Part III.
Toward Better Relationships

Bowen quotes from Bowen, M.: *Family Therapy in Clinical Practice,* Jason Aronson, New York, 1978, pp. 371, 495.

Chapter 16.—Growing a Self

Bowen quotes from Bowen, M.: *Family Therapy in Clinical Practice,* Jason Aronson, New York, 1978, pp. 316, 317, 371, 540.

The apt term "growing a self" was used in clinical supervisory sessions with Kathleen Kerr.

Chapter 17.—Managing the Emotional Self in Relationships

Bowen quote from "An Odyssey Toward Science," the epilogue of *Family Evaluation* by Michael Kerr and Murray Bowen, New York, Norton and Co., 1988, p. 360.

Bowen quotes from Bowen, N.: *Family Therapy in Clinical Practice,* Jason Aronson, New York, 1978, pp. 362, 495.

Elmer Green quote from "Some Historical Notes on the Biofeed-back Research Society: Leading to Its Formation in October 1969," *Biofeedback,* Winter 1989.

The work of pioneers in the field, Dr. Elmer and Alyce Green, is important. Especially: Elmer Green, "Biofeedback, Consciousness and Human Potential," *Perkins Journal,* Vol. 39, April 1986; and Elmer Green and Alyce Green, "General and Specific Applications of Thermal Biofeedback," and *Biofeedback: Principles and Practice for Clinicians,* 2nd edition, edited by Basmajian, Williams and Wilkins, 1983, Chapter 15.

Biofeedback training and its possibilities with special reference to relationships were presented in papers from biofeedback conferences "Physiology and Relationships," held at the Georgetown University Family Center over several years. These are available on audiotape.

I am especially indebted, for whatever beginner's experiential and theoretical understanding of biofeedback I may have to my coaches, friends and colleagues, Mrs. Louise Rauseo and Mrs. Priscilla Friesen Felton.

Chapter 18.—Processing Feelings and Dealing With Crisis

Bowen quotes from Bowen, M.: *Family Therapy in Clinical Practice,* Jason Aronson, New York, 1978, pp. 292, 422.

Many years ago I attended a meeting of psychiatry alumni at my residency training alma mater, the University of Buffalo, where the useful idea of crisis was presented as "a period of rapid change" during which people can increase or decrease their functioning permanently. The identity of the presenter is unknown.

Chapter 19.—Ten Misconceptions That Can Defeat a Relationship and Ten Ways to Promote Success

Bowen quotes from Bowen, M.: *Family Therapy in Clinical Practice,* Jason Aronson, New York, 1978, pp. 363, 364.

Chapter 20.—Living Out the Theory

Most of these ideas have grown out of my own attempts to apply theory in my own life as well as in situations presented to me through the years in clinical practice.

"That which can be created in a relationship can be changed in a relationship," is quoted from Dr. Michael Kerr, in a clinical conference, quoting Dr. Bowen, 1991.

—Friendships

On friendship systems, Dr. Walter Toman's recent work in this area, presented at the Georgetown University Symposium, 1986, is of interest.

My own thinking in this, as in so many areas of theory, has also been catalyzed by my own friendships, especially my friendship with Carroll Hoskins Michaels, M.S.W. Her extensive work in Bowen family systems theory has been stimulating and challenging to me from the beginning.

—Love Relationships

Bowen quote from Bowen, M.: *Family Therapy in Clinical Practice,* Jason Aronson, New York, 1978, p. 540.

—Parents and Children

Bowen quote from Bowen, M.: *Family Therapy in Clinical Practice,* Jason Aronson, New York, 1978, p. 297.

—Divorce

Bowen quote from Bowen, M.: *Family Therapy in Clinical Practice,* Jason Aronson, New York, 1978, p. 535.

Recommended reading is *Adult Children of Divorce* by Edward Beal, M.D. Dr. Beal is a long-time colleague of Dr. Bowen and a faculty member at Georgetown Family Center.

—The Single Life

Bowen quote from Bowen, M.: *Family Therapy in Clinical Practice,* Jason Aronson, New York, 1978, p. 536.

—Professional Relationships

Bowen quote from Bowen, M.: *Family Therapy in Clinical Practice,* Jason Aronson, New York, 1978, pp. 309, 310.

—Workplace Relationships

Bowen quote from "An Odyssey Toward Science," the epilogue of *Family Evaluation* by Michael Kerr and Murray Bowen, Norton and Co., New York, 1988, p. 373.

The Georgetown Family Center publication on this subject, "Understanding Organizations," grew out of a conference on the subject, facilitated by Kathleen Wiseman.

Dr. Donald Shoulberg, Menninger Family Center, Prairie Village, Kansas, stimulated much thinking for me in this area, as he did in many areas.

—Societal Process and International Relationships

Bowen quote from "An Odyssey Toward Science," the epilogue of *Family Evaluation* by Michael Kerr and Murray Bowen, Norton and Co., New York, 1988, p. 385.

Also, Bowen, M.: *Family Therapy in Clinical Practice,* Jason Aronson, New York, 1978, p. 279.

Calhoun's work has been explicated in many lectures at the Georgetown University Family Center by Dr. Calhoun and other faculty members, especially Dr. Roberta Holt and Dr. Daniel Papero.

Other Books About Bowen Family Systems Theory

Hall, Margaret: *Bowen Family Systems Theory and Its Uses,* Jason Aronson, New York. A sociologist's perspective.

Kerr, M.E., and Bowen, M: *Family Evaluation,* W. W. Norton and Co., New York, 1988. Written for therapists but being read by many others as well.

Papero, D. V.: *Bowen Family Systems Theory,* Allyn and Bacon, Needham Heights, MA, 1990.

Appendix I

Glossary

Anxiety.—Usually defined as response of the organism to real or imagined threat. Clinical experience at some levels of differentiation suggests that anxiety is so continuously present in life, so much a fact of the individual's and family's patterns, as to not necessarily need to be stimulated by real or imagined threat. For that reason, another definition might be proposed; simply *heightened reactivity*. Anxiety may be a reaction to stressors from outside the family system or the person or it may be generated from inside the system or from within the person. It may be chronic, being passed along in a family system for years, or generations, or it may be acute— that is, relatively short-term. The effects of anxiety in a system are multiple: generally an increase in togetherness is evidenced by more triangling and other relationship postures. Physical, mental, emotional, or social symptoms of any intensity can occur at any level of differentiation, given enough anxiety. Anxiety is manifest in quantitative changes in the body that include cells, organs, and organ systems, as well as thought and behavior expressions and patterns.

Basic Self.—The core of the self, made up of all that guides and determines the course of the self. It is partly automatic, or emotional, and partly thoughtful. The thoughtful part of basic self is derived from and indistinguishable from a conscious set of principles. These principles can be seen as an inner guidance system. Basic self is non-negotiable; that is, it is not given up to a relationship, nor is it added to by a relationship. Because of that, it is thought to have boundaries that are not "permeable." It is distinguished from the pseudo, or functional, self, which, because of its more permeable boundaries, can be given up to added to in relationships. The functional self functions better in favorable circumstances—less well in adverse conditions. Basic self, because of its inner guidance system and less permeable boundaries, is reliable in all kinds of circumstances. People higher on the scale of differentiation have more basic self, whereas people lower on the scale have less basic self.

Differentiation of Self.—The cornerstone of Bowen family systems theory, and the continuing project of people who work with the theory. The word "differentiation" derives from the science of embryology. In the developing fetus groups of cells that are identical in the beginning become different from each other. They "differentiate" in order to form the different organs of the body. The concept as applied to the self describes the variation that exists among people in their abilities to adapt—that is, to deal with the exigencies of life and to reach their goals. People fall along a theoretical spectrum of differentiation, depending on their unresolved emotional attachment to the family of origin. Indices of differentiation include physical health and abilities as well as intelligence, social skills, and emotional maturity. People range from very high levels of differentiation of self to very low levels, depending on how much basic self is present. People at higher levels, those with more basic self, tend toward more overall success in life, both vocationally and in their relationships. They also tend towards less physical, mental/emotional, and social illnesses. The more basic self a person attains, the more inner direction he or she has, and the more choice at any given time regarding whether to operate out of emotions or intellect. People at higher levels function more often out of their principles, which are well thought out, than do people at lower levels. They have more choice between their thinking and feeling functions. People at lower levels have less choice between feeling and thinking functions; their behavior patterns tend to be emotion-based and more automatic. Emotion-based patterns include compliance, rebelliousness, and fear of rejection. Lower level individuals also have more attachment needs than do those at higher levels. Differentiation of self has a rough equivalence with emotional maturity, but the two ideas are somewhat different, since differentiation has nothing to do with chronological age, which is sometimes linked to emotional maturity. Differentiation is a much broader concept than emotional maturity, taking in all the areas of functioning of an individual, including the physical health. The concept contains within it a set of rather detailed principles, which, when implemented, lead not only to improved emotional and relationship functioning, but also improved functioning in the intellectual, social, and physical spheres. There is a directly proportional relationship between level of differentiation and amount of basic self. At higher levels of differentiation, a greater amount of basic self has been developed; at lower levels, a smaller amount. Level of differentiation can be properly assessed only by years of observation, and by taking into consideration the levels of differentiation of important others. A given individual of an emotional system may be doing well, but only at the expense of the functioning of others in the system. The effect of circumstances is easier to observe on the functional self than on the basic self.

Emotional Maturity.—The ability of the individual to manage the emotional part of the self in an adaptive way—a way in which long-term benefits override short-term benefits when the two conflict. A similar concept to differentiation of self, it is not as inclusive. *(See also Differentiation of Self.)*

Emotional System.—The emotional unit, a group of individuals who, by virtue of time spent together are involved in meaningful relationships. This might be a herd of animals, a human family (nuclear or extended), or a workplace system. Emotions or feelings circuit from individual to individual by means of patterned emotional reactions— distance, conflict, overfunctioning/underfunctioning—or triangling.

This term may also refer to the emotional system within an individual; that is, the part of the nervous system and organs involved in emotional responses: For instance, a perception of danger may involve sense organs, such as eyes and ears, reptilian or limbic brain, hypothalamus alerting adrenals, adrenal glands secreting adrenalin, which raises blood pressure and increases cardiac output, as well as many other physiologic responses that make a fight or flight response more efficient.

Emotions.—The instinctual forces that operate in animals, and thus, in human beings. Examples of these forces are territoriality and procreation, found in reptiles as well as more complex species, or nurturance of young, and play, found only in higher mammals. These reactions have an insistent quality. They originate in the various parts of the midbrain associated with these functions and are carried out by the individual's "emotional system," the brain-nervous system-muscle or other end organ involved in the emotion. Emotions also include fight or flight reactions and patterned reactions, which get set in the developing organism over time with repetition.

Feelings.—Pleasure or pain experiences of varying degrees of intensity. Originating in the emotional system of the individual, they are emotions the individual is aware of.

Functional Self.—*See Basic Self*

Fusion.—Emotional attachment of two or more selfs for which the mother/child symbiosis is a paradigm; can be seen in any intense or primary relationship. Both selfs in a fusion are intensely emotionally reactive to each other and experience a loss or gain of self in the relationship.

Inner Guidance System.—*See Basic Self*

Nuclear Family Emotional System.—*See Emotional System*

Pseudo self.—The part of self that is negotiated in a relationship. (*See also Basic Self*)

Reactivity.—The tendency of the organism to respond to perceived threat or the anxiety of others.

Scale of Differentiation.—An imaginary continuum upon which all human beings fall, from the most differentiated to the least. This scale does not exist in actuality and will probably never be developed because of the broadness of the concept of differentiation. It is necessary to evaluate for differentiation over time as well as across the relationship system of any individual. *(See also Differentiation)*

Self.—*See Basic Self*

Symbiosis.—A mutually dependent emotional attachment between two people. The concept comes from biology where two organisms are dependent upon each other for survival. The human, for example, lives in symbiosis with certain bacteria present in the gastrointestinal tract. The bacteria produce vitamin K, essential for the clotting of human blood. In the family, individuals who fuse selfs into relationships emotionally can be thought of as being in an emotional symbiosis. To the degree that the symbiosis is resolved, the individual is said to have differentiated self. To the degree the original tendency toward symbiosis remains, differentiation of self is incomplete, and the self is vulnerable to forming other emotionally dependent relationships.

System.—The emotional relationships between or among human beings or other animals. Usually all that is needed for individuals to become emotionally significant, or related, is for them to spend a significant amount of time with one another. When individuals spend a significant amount of time with one another, they will begin, sooner or later, to trigger each other emotionally, and the phenomenon of "passing" emotions from one to another, in patterns, can be observed. *(See also Emotional system)*

Triangle.—Three individuals emotionally related to each other—the building block of emotional systems. Emotional intensity takes place alternately among the different pairs forming the triangle; anxiety travels around it. In each family system there are many triangles, some of which reach out to society at large. In this way, society itself is built of interlocking triangles.

Appendix II

Differentiation of Self Scale

Dr. Bowen wrote several times of the differences in lives lived at different levels on the hypothetical scale of differentiation. Here is one of his descriptions, written in 1971.

"Differentiation of Self Scale. This scale is a way of evaluating all people on a single continuum, from the lowest to the highest possible level of human functioning. The scale ranges from 0 to 100. . . .

"At the lowest point on the scale is the lowest possible level of self or the greatest degree of no-self or undifferentiation. At the highest point on the scale is a postulated level of complete differentiation of perfect self, which man has not yet achieved. The level of differentiation is the degree to which one self fuses or merges into another self in a close emotional relationship. The scale eliminated the concept of normal, which has been elusive for psychiatry.

"The scale has nothing to do with emotional illness or psychopathology. There are low-scale people who manage to keep their lives in emotional equilibrium without developing emotional illness, and there are higher-scale people who can develop severe symptoms under great stress. However, lower-scale people are vulnerable to stress and are much more prone to illness, including physical and social illness, and their dysfunction is more likely to become chronic when it does occur. Higher-scale people can recover emotional equilibrium quickly after the stress passes.

"Two levels of self have been postulated. One is solid self, made up of firmly held convictions and beliefs. It is formed slowly and can be changed from within self, but it is never changed by coercion or persuasion by others. The other level of self is the pseudo-self, made up of knowledge incorporated by the intellect and of principles and beliefs acquired from others. The pseudo-self is acquired from others, and it is negotiable in relationship with others. It can be changed by emotional pressure to enhance one's image with others or to oppose the other.

"In the average person, the level of solid self is relatively low in comparison with the level of pseudo-self. A pseudo-self can function well in most relationships. But in an intense emotional relationship, such as marriage, the pseudo-self of one merges with the pseudo-self of the other. One becomes the functional self and the other a functional no-self. The emotional interplay in fusion states, the undifferentiated family ego mass, is the subject of much of the dynamics in a family emotional system.

"Low-scale people live in a feeling world in which they cannot distinguish feeling from fact. So much life energy goes into seeking love or approval or in attacking the other for not providing it that there is no energy for developing a self or for goal-directed activity. The lives of low-scale people are totally relationship-oriented. Major life decisions are based on what feels right. A low-scale person with a life in reasonable asymptomatic adjustment is one who is able to keep the feeling system in equilibrium by giving and receiving love and by the sharing of self with others. Low-scale people do so much borrowing and trading of self and show such wide fluctuations in their functioning levels of self that it is difficult to estimate their basic levels of self except over long periods of time.

"As a group, low-scale people have a high incidence of human problems. Relationships are tenuous, and a new problem can arise in an unsuspected area even while they are trying to deal with the previous problem. When the relationship equilibrium fails, the family goes into functional collapse, with illness or other problems. They can be too numb to feel, and there is no longer any energy to seek love and approval. So much energy is devoted to the discomfort of the moment that they live from day to day. At the very lowest point on the scale are those too impaired to live outside an institution.

"People in the 25-to-50 segment of the scale also live in a feeling-dominated world, but the fusion of selfs is less intense, and there is increasing capacity to differentiate a self. Major life decisions are based on what feels right rather than on principle, much life energy goes into seeking love and approval, and there is little energy for goal-directed activity.

"Those in the 35-to-40 range present some of the best examples of a feeling-oriented life. They are removed from the impairment and life paralysis that characterize the lower-scale people, and the feeling orientation is more clearly seen. They are sensitized to emotional disharmony, to the opinions of others, and to creating a good impression. They are apt students of facial expressions, gestures, tones of voice, and actions that may mean approval or disapproval. Success in school or at work is determined more by approval from important others than by the basic value of the work. Their spirits can soar with expressions of love and approval or be dashed by the lack of it. These are people with low levels of solid self but reasonable levels of pseudo-self, which is obtained from and is negotiable in the relationship system.

"People in the upper part of the 25-to-50 segment of the scale have some awareness of intellectual principles, but the system is still so fused with feeling that the budding self is expressed in dogmatic authoritativeness, in the compliance of a disciple, or in the opposition of a rebel. Some of those in this group use intellect in the service of the relationship system. As children, their academic prowess won them approval. They lack their own convictions and beliefs, but they are quick to know the thoughts and feelings of others, and their knowledge provides them with a facile pseudo-self. If the relationship system approves, they can be brilliant students and disciples. If their expectations are not met, they assemble a pseudo-self in point by point opposition to the established order.

"People in the 50-to-60 segment of the scale are aware of the difference between feelings and intellectual principle, but they are still so responsive to the relationship system that they hesitate to say what they believe, lest they offend the listener.

"People still higher on the scale are operationally clear about the differences between feelings and intellect, and they are free to state beliefs calmly, without attacking the beliefs of others for the enhancement of self and without having to defend themselves against the attacks of others. They are sufficiently free of the control of the feeling system to have a choice between intimate emotional closeness and goal-directed activity, and they can derive satisfaction and pleasure from either. They have a realistic appraisal of self to others, in contrast to lower-scale people, who feel self to be the center of the universe and who either overvalue or devalue self.

"The differentiation of self scale is important as a theoretical concept for viewing the total human phenomenon in perspective. It is valuable in estimating the over-all potential of people and in making predictions about the general pattern of their lives. But it is not useful in making month to month or even year to year evaluations of scale levels. There is so much trading and borrowing and negotiating for pseudo-self in the relationship system, especially in the lower half of the scale, and such wide functional shifts in the level of self that it is difficult to estimate scale levels on short-term information.

"Most people spend their lives at the same basic level they had when they left their parental families. They consolidate this level in a marriage, after which there are few life experiences that change this basic level. Many life experiences automatically raise or lower the functioning levels of self, but this shift can be as easily lost as gained. There are calculated ways to raise the basic level of self, but doing so is a monumental life task, and it is easy for one to say that the possible gain is not worth the effort. The method of psychotherapy described here is directed at helping families differentiate a few points higher on the scale."

In 1972, Bowen wrote:

"People in the lower half of the scale live in a 'feeling' controlled world in which feelings and subjectivity are dominant over the objective reasoning process most of the time. They do not distinguish feeling from fact and major life decisions are based on what 'feels' right. Primary life goals are oriented around love, happiness, comfort, and security; these goals come closest to fulfillment when relationships with others are in equilibrium. So much life energy goes into seeking love and approval, or attacking the other for not providing it, that there is little energy left for self-determined, goal-directed activity . . . . An important life principle is 'giving and receiving' love, attention, and approval. Life can stay in symptom-free adjustment as long as the relationship system is in comfortable equilibrium. Discomfort and anxiety occur with events that disrupt or threaten the relationship equilibrium. Chronic disruption of the relationship system results in dysfunction and a high incidence of human problems, including physical and emotional illness and social dysfunction. People in the upper half of the scale have an increasingly defined level of basic self and less pseudo-self. Each person is more of an autonomous self: there is less emotional fusion in close relationships, less energy is needed to maintain self in the fusions, more energy is available for goal-directed activity, and more satisfaction is derived from directed activity. Moving into the upper half of the scale one finds people who have an increasing capacity to differentiate between feelings and objective reality. For instance, people in the 50-to-75 range of the scale have increasingly defined convictions and opinions on most essential issues but they are still sensitive to opinions of those about them and some decisions are based on feelings in order not to risk the disapproval of important others.

"According to the theory, there is some degree of fusion in close relationships, and some degree of an 'undifferentiated family ego mass' at every scale level below 100. When the scale was first devised, the 100 level was reserved for the being who was perfect in all levels of emotional, cellular, and physiological functioning. I expected there might be some unusual figures in history, or possibly some living persons who would fit into the mid-90 range. Increasing experience with the scale indicates that all people have areas of good functioning and essential areas in which life functioning is poor. . .my impression is that 75 is a very high-level person and that those above 60 constitute a small percentage of society.

"The characteristics of high-scale people convey an important aspect of the concept. They are operationally clear about the difference between feeling and thinking. . . . The relative separation of feelings and thinking brings life much more under the control of deliberate thoughts, in contrast to low-scale people whose life is a pawn of the ebb and flow of the emotional process. In relationships with others, high-scale people are free to engage in goal-directed activity, or to lose 'self' in the intimacy of a close relationship, in contrast to low-scale people who either have to avoid relationships lest they slip automatically into an uncomfortable fusion, or have no choice but continued pursuit of a close relationship for gratification of emotional 'needs.' The high-scale person is less reactive to praise or criticism and he has a more realistic evaluation of his own self in contrast to the lower-level person whose evaluation is either far above or far below reality . . . .

". . . A detailed history of functional shifts within a family over a period of years can convey a fairly accurate pattern of the family members in relation to each other. . . . The life style of a person at one level is so different from someone only a few points removed on the scale that they do not choose each other for personal relationships. There are many life experiences that can raise or lower the *functioning* levels of self, but few that can change the basic level of differentiation acquired while people are still with their parental families. Unless there is some unusual circumstance, the basic level from their parental family is consolidated in a marriage, following which the only shift is a functional shift. The functional shifts can be striking. For example, a wife who had a functional level at marriage equal to her husband's may become de-selfed to the point of chronic alcoholism. She then functions far below her original level while the husband functions equally far above his original level. Many of these functional levels are sufficiently consolidated so that they can appear much like basic levels to the inexperienced."

By 1976 the concept was fleshed out even further.

"At the fusion end of the spectrum, the intellect is so flooded by emotionality that the total life course is determined by the emotional process . . . rather than beliefs or opinions. The intellect exists as an appendage of the feeling system. It may function reasonably well in mathematics or physics, or in impersonal areas, but on personal subjects its functioning is controlled by the emotions. The emotional system is hypothesized to be part of the instinctual forces that govern automatic functions. The human is adept at explanations to emphasize that he is different from lower forms of life, and at denying his relation with nature. The emotional system operates with predictable, knowable stimuli that govern the instinctual behavior in all forms of life. The more a life is governed by the emotional system, the more it follows the course of all instinctual behavior, in spite of intellectualized explanations to the contrary. At higher levels of differentiation, the function of the emotional and intellectual systems are more clearly distinguishable. There are the same automatic emotional forces that govern instinctual behavior, but intellect is sufficiently autonomous for logical reasoning and decisions based on thinking. When I first began to present this concept, I used the term undifferentiated family ego mass to describe the emotional 'stuck togetherness' in families. Although this phrase was an assemblage of words from conventional theory, and thus did not conform to the plan to use concepts consistent with biology, it fairly accurately described emotional fusion. . . .

"The most common criticism was that a differentiated person appeared to be cold, distant, rigid, and nonfeeling. It is difficult for professional people to grasp the notion of differentiation when they have spent their working lives believing that the free expression of feelings represents a high level of functioning and intellectualization represents an unhealthy defense against it. . . . A poorly differentiated person is trapped within a feeling world. . . . A segment of these . . . people use random, inconsistent, intellectual-sounding verbalization to explain away their plight. A more differentiated person can participate freely in the emotional sphere without the fear of becoming too fused with others. He is also free to shift to calm, logical reasoning for decisions that govern his life. The logical intellectual process is quite different from the inconsistent, intellectualized verbalizations of the emotionally fused person. . . .

". . . The schematic framework and the use of the term scale resulted in hundreds of letters requesting copies of 'the scale.' Most who wrote had not grasped the concept nor the variables that govern the functional levels of differentiation . . . . The theoretical concept is most important. It eliminates the barriers between schizophrenia, neurosis, and normal; it also transcends categories such as genius, social class, and cultural-ethnic differences. It applies to all human forms of life. It might even apply to subhuman forms if we only knew enough. . . .

". . . In periods of emotional intimacy, two pseudo-selfs will fuse into each other, one losing self to the other, who gains self. The solid self does not participate in the fusion phenomenon. The solid self says, 'This is who I am, what I believe, what I stand for, and what I will do or will not do,' in a given situation. The solid self is made up of clearly defined beliefs, opinions, convictions, and life principles. These are incorporated into self from one's own life experiences, by a process of intellectual reasoning and the careful consideration of the alternatives involved in the choice. . . .Each belief and life principle is consistent with all the others, and self will take action on the principles even in situations of high anxiety and duress. . . . .

"The pseudo-self is created by emotional pressure, and it can be modified by emotional pressure. Every emotional unit, whether it be the family or the total of society, exerts pressure on group members to conform to the ideals and principles of the group. The pseudo-self is composed of a vast assortment of principles, beliefs, philosophies, and knowledge acquired because it is required or considered right by the group. Since the principles are acquired under pressure, they are random and inconsistent with one another, without the individual's being aware of the discrepancy. Pseudo-self is appended onto the self, in contrast to solid self which is incorporated into self after careful, logical reasoning. The pseudo-self is a 'pretend' self. It was acquired to conform to the environment and it contains discordant and assorted principles that pretend to be in emotional harmony with a variety of social groups, institutions, businesses, political parties, and religious groups, without self's being aware that the groups are inconsistent with each other. The joining of groups is motivated more by the relationship system than the principle involved. . . . The solid self is intellectually aware of the inconsistency between the groups, and the decision to join or reject membership is an intellectual process based on careful weighing of the advantages and disadvantages.

"The pseudo-self is an actor and can be many different selfs. The list of pretends is extensive. He can pretend to be more important or less important, stronger or weaker, or more attractive or less attractive than is realistic. . . . The level of solid self is stable. The pseudo-self is unstable, and it responds to a variety of social pressures and stimuli. The pseudo-self was acquired at the behest of the relationship system, and it is negotiable in the relationship system. . . .

". . . I believe that the level of solid self is lower, and of the pseudo-self . . . higher in all of us than most are aware. It is the pseudo-self that is involved in fusion and the many ways of giving, receiving, lending, borrowing, trading, and exchanging of self. In any exchange, one gives up a little self to the other, each is trying to be the way the other wants self to be, and each in turn makes demands on the other to be different. This is pretending and trading in pseudo-self. In a marriage, two pseudo-selfs fuse into a we-ness in which one becomes the dominant decision maker or the most active in taking initiative for the we-ness. The dominant one gains self at the expense of the other, who loses it. The adaptive one may volunteer to give up self to the dominant one, who accepts it; or the exchange may be worked out after bargaining. The more the spouses can alternate these roles, the healthier the marriage. The exchanging of selves may be on a short- or long-term basis. The borrowing and trading of selves may take place automatically in a work group in which the emotional process ends up with one employee in the one-down or de-selfed position, while the others gain self. This exchanging of pseudo-self is an automatic emotional process that occurs as people manipulate each other in subtle life postures. The exchanges can be brief—for instance, criticism that makes one feel bad for a few days; or it can be a long-term process in which the adaptive spouse becomes so de-selfed, he or she is no longer able to make decisions and collapses in selfless dysfunction—psychosis or chronic physical illness. These mechanisms are much less intense in better levels of differentiation or when anxiety is low, but the process of people losing and gaining self in an emotional network is so complex and the degree of shifts so great that it is impossible to estimate functional levels of differentiation except from following a life pattern over long periods.

"Profile of low levels of differentiation . . . . they say 'I feel that . . . .' when it would be accurate to express an opinion or belief. They consider it truthful and sincere to say, 'I feel,' and false and insincere to express an opinion from themselves. They spend their lives in a day to day struggle to keep the relationship system in balance, or in an effort to achieve some degree of comfort and freedom from anxiety. They are incapable of making long-term goals except in vague terms, such as 'I want to be successful, or happy, or have a good job, or have security.' They grow up as dependent appendages of their parents, following which they seek other equally dependent relationships in which they can borrow enough strength to function. A no-self person who is adept at pleasing his boss may make a better employee than one who has a self. This group is made up of people preoccupied with

keeping their dependent relationships in harmony, people who have failed and who go from one symptomatic crisis to another, and people who have given up in the futile effort to adapt. . . .

"Profile of moderate levels of differentiation of self. . . . life styles are more flexible than the lower levels of differentiation. When anxiety is low, functioning can resemble good levels of differentiation. When anxiety is high, functioning can resemble that of low levels of differentiation. Lives are relationship oriented, and major life energy goes to loving and being loved, and seeking approval from others. Feelings are more openly expressed than in lower level people. Life energy is directed more to what others think and to winning friends and approval than to goal-directed activity. Self esteem is dependent on others. It can soar to heights with a compliment or be crushed by criticism. Success in school is oriented more to learning the system and to pleasing the teacher than to the primary goal of learning. Success in business or in social life depends more on pleasing the boss or the social leader, and more on who one knows and gaining relationship status than in the inherent value of their work. . . . Lacking a solid self-conviction about the world's knowledge, they use pseudo-self statements, such as 'The rule says . . .' or 'Science has proved . . .' taking information out of context to make their points. They may have enough free-functioning intellect to have mastered academic knowledge about impersonal things . . . . However, intellect about personal matters is lacking and their personal lives are in chaos.

"The pseudo-self may be a conforming disciple who pretends to be in harmony with a particular philosophy or set of principles or, when frustrated, he can assume the opposite posture as a rebel or revolutionary person. The rebel is lacking a self of his own. His pseudo-self posture is merely the exact opposite of the majority viewpoint. The revolutionary person is against the prevailing system, but he has nothing to offer in its place. The sameness of polarized opposites in emotional situations has led me to define revolution as a convulsion that prevents change. It is relationship-oriented energy that goes back and forth on the same points, the issue of each side being determined by the position of the other; neither is capable of a position not determined by the other.

"People in the moderate range of differentiation have the most intense versions of overt feeling. . . . They are in a lifelong pursuit of the ideal close relationship. When closeness is achieved, it increases the emotional fusion to which they react with distance and alienation, which can then stimulate another closeness cycle. Failing to achieve closeness, they may go to withdrawal and depression, or to pursuit of closeness in another relationship. . . .

"Profile of moderate to good differentiation of self. These are the people with enough basic differentiation between the emotional and intellectual systems for the two systems to function alongside each other as a cooperative team. The intellectual system . . . can hold its own and function autonomously without being dominated by the emotional system when anxiety increases. Above 50 . . . has learned that the emotional system runs an effective course in most areas of functioning, but in critical situations the automatic emotional decisions create long-term complications for the total organism. People above 50 have developed a reasonable level of solid self on most of the essential issues in life. In periods of calm, they have employed logical reasoning to develop beliefs, principles, and convictions that they use to overrule the emotional system in situations of anxiety and panic . . . . People at the lower part of this group are those who know there is a better way; but . . . they end up following life courses similar to those below 50.

"People in the upper part of this group are those in whom there is more solid self . . . no longer a prisoner of the emotional-feeling world. They are able to live more freely and to have more satisfying emotional lives within the emotional system. They can participate fully in emotional events knowing they can extricate themselves with logical reasoning when the need arises. There may be periods . . . in which they permit the automatic pilot of the emotional system to have full control, but when trouble develops they can take over, calm the anxiety, and avoid a life crisis. . . . They are not unaware of the relationship system, but their life courses can be determined more from within themselves than from what others think. . . . They marry spouses with equal levels of differentiation. The lifestyle of a spouse at another level would be sufficiently different to be considered emotionally incompatible. The marriage is a functioning partnership. The spouses can enjoy the full range of emotional intimacy without either being de-selfed by the other. They can be autonomous selfs together or alone . . . . Spouses . . . can permit their children to grow and develop their own autonomous selfs without undue anxiety or without trying to fashion their children in their own images. The spouses and the children are each more responsible for themselves, and do not have to blame others for failures or credit anyone else for their successes. People with better levels of differentiation are able to function well with other people, or alone, as the situation may require. Their lives are more orderly, they are able to cope successfully with a broader range of human situations, and they are remarkably free from the full range of human problems . . . .

". . . A common mistake is to equate the better differentiated person with a 'rugged individualist.' I consider rugged individualism to be the exaggerated pretend posture of a person struggling against emotional fusion. The differentiated person is always aware of others and the relationship system around him. There are so many forces and counterforces and details in differentiation that one has to get a broad panoramic view of the total human phenomenon in order to be able to see differentiation. Once it is possible to see the phenomenon, there it is, operating in full view, right in front of our eyes. Once it is possible to see the phenomenon, it is then possible to apply the concept to hundreds of different human situations. To try to apply it without knowing it is an exercise in futility."

Appendix III

Toman's Sibling Positions

Position Portraits

Following is a condensed version of the sibling-position portraits as Dr. Walter Toman originally described them.

It should be noted, also, that much of personality development has to do with parents' sibling positions. The parents' personality characteristics, in large part derived from their own sibling positions, become important determining factors in personality development. The way parents relate to their children has a great deal to do with the relationships they formed with their siblings. For example, a youngest brother of brothers, as a father, may tend to relate more easily to his older son who is an older brother of brothers, just as he had at an earlier time of his life related to his own older brother. This relationship will then have a bearing on his oldest son's personality development, and will possibly be a different relationship than the father will have with his other children. The personality development of all siblings will be differentially affected by their parents' sibling position. This is part of the answer to the question, "How can people reared by the same parents turn out so differently?"

In trying to determine characteristics of individuals in the middle of a large family, see "The Middle Child" (page 206) for an explanation of how to use this guide.

The Oldest Brother of Brothers

The oldest brother of brothers finds it easy to assume responsibility for other people, especially men. He is nurturing and caring of the group he assumes responsibility for and expects loyalty and trust in return. He accepts authority easily, but may become bossy. He easily knows and implements the ingredients of achievement. He is sensitive and shy around women. He is attracted to the youngest sister of either brothers or sisters. An oldest sister of brothers could also please him if she does not mother him. An oldest sister of sisters would be a difficult match for him because of her similar tendency to lock horns when it comes to leadership. He is most likely to choose women of the same sibling position as that of his mother. His marriage will do better if he is permitted to maintain male friendships. He is a concerned and responsible father if he does not become too strict, controlling, or uninvolved. He will tend to have friendships among several sibling positions, but may clash with friends who are also older brothers.

The Youngest Brother of Brothers

The youngest brother of brothers is more of a follower and leans especially on men. He works well with men who appreciate and respect him and enjoys being understood by other men. He does not really enjoy being a leader. He may be obstinate, daring, bold, and complaining. Physically strong, he is kind-hearted and soft. He is not as interested in achievement and acquisition as in quality of life and the joys of the moment. He is not goal- or content-oriented, but if not tied to routine work, he may accomplish great and unusual things, especially in scientific, technical, or artistic fields. With women he is soft, yielding, and faithful, if unpredictable. His best partner would be the oldest sister of brothers or sisters or the youngest sister of brothers. His poorest match would be with the youngest sister of sisters or an only child. He too will want to continue contact with his male friends. He is a good companion to his children, as a father, but may tend to relate in the family too much as a child. Best friends tend to become oldest brothers of brothers or middle brothers who had younger brothers or only children whose fathers were oldest siblings.

Oldest Brother of Sisters

The oldest brother of sisters understands, appreciates, and works well with women. He does not refuse leadership roles but also does not seek them out. He is not susceptible to male chauvinism and is not one to join male clubs. He is not obsessed with work, maintaining a live-and-let-live philosophy. Materialism is not one of his vices. He will make sacrifices for the woman in his life. His best partner would be the youngest sister of brothers. The oldest sister of brothers may mother him too much, and he shows little attraction for oldest sisters of sisters. He is a good father, concerned about his children and willing to be actively involved with them, but he does not become consumed with worry over his children, since to him, his wife is the most important person in the family. Male friends interest him little and in groups he is somewhat neutral and detached.

Youngest Brother of Sisters

The youngest brother of sisters, without trying, attracts solicitation, care, and services from women around him. He was valued and privileged by his parents, and he tends to keep that position as he goes through life in his relationships at work and in the family. He can assume leadership roles easily, especially with feminine support, but his male colleagues may be skeptical. He has a well-developed ability to charm women but really doesn't understand them, feeling he himself is all that they should really need. His best partner is an older sister of brothers. An oldest sister of sisters seems self-righteous and strict to him. A youngest sister of brothers seems not motherly enough and too dependent. A youngest sister of sisters seems too impulsive and ambitious. He is not especially keen to be a father but indulges his wife her wishes. He may experience some jealousy of his wife's attention to the children. He is both companion and advisor to the children. He may tend to grant them too much freedom and independence. He is less interested in male friends than other men.

Male Only Child

The male only child is used to living with considerably older people and tends to prefer having older people around him throughout his life, wanting to be loved, nurtured, and supported by them. He is quite convinced of his own importance in the scheme of things. Because he received more attention and stimulation from his parents than other children, as a rule he usually had an edge in intelligence and talent as he was growing up. That edge, combined with encouragement from parents, guardians, and teachers may stimulate him to rise to great heights of accomplishments in his chosen field. He may even have a position of leadership although he is not gifted in the area. He is motivated more by the enjoyment of life, art, intellectual and cultural exchanges than by materialism, but his greatest and natural motivation is to become the focus of attention. In love matches, he is most attracted to oldest sisters of brother and also oldest sisters of sisters, women a few years older than he or persons with similar or identical sibling position as his mother. He may get along with a younger sister if she is considerably younger than he is. Marriage to another only child creates difficulties in that the two are unable to live up to each other's unconscious expectations for attention. He is not particularly motivated to be a father and may have some feelings of jealousy for the child, but in the end may pamper or overprotect his child. Male friends are less important to him than father figures.

Oldest Sister of Sisters

The oldest sister of sisters is a caretaker and order-giver. She likes to be in charge, and derives her leadership position from another person in authority, often an older man or a man in a high position, like her father. She can remain unquestionably devoted to an older man of authority for long periods of her life. Material wealth and goods are less important to her than responsibility and power. She may seem intimidating to men who want to court her. It is hard for her to give in. A most amiable partner is the youngest brother of sisters, but she may criticize him for being soft or sloppy. A youngest brother of brothers will also be compatible. An oldest brother of sisters seems to conceited to her, because of his experience with other women, and she will find it hard to be emotionally intimate with an oldest brother of brothers. An only child could be her partner if he is flexible. She is most interested in men who held the same sibling position her father held. Children are more important to her than her husband, but the arrival of children may relieve any tensions existing in the marriage. Her need for authority and nurturing now has a more natural outlet. She may become overprotective and smothering to some extent. She loves the dependence of children. She may suffer from the empty-nest syndrome when they leave. At the same time, she may find it easier to forego marriage and family life altogether than other women do. Women friends are more important to her than men friends. She will experience a need to continue her contacts with women through the years, and her favorite friends will usually be a younger sister of sisters. Other compatible friendship relationships for her include only children, especially if they are a few years younger than she is or are daughters of mothers who are youngest sisters. She also understands other oldest sisters of sisters although these may not be close friendships.

The Youngest Sister of Sisters

The youngest sister of sisters is bubbly and impulsive, loving change and excitement. She is attractive and may find herself in competition with other women. She can be moody and capricious. She balks if someone tries to manipulate her. She will work hard for recognition and praise, loving to excel. She seeks guidance from other people, but not overtly. She is on a lifelong search for respect and can be quite sensitive about this. She tends to be suggestible but has the courage to take great risks. While she is interested in material things, she may be inconsistent in her efforts to amass things. She is ambivalent regarding men. While it is easy for her to attract men, she may become competitive, especially if a man shows any tendency to take charge. Her best partner is an older brother of sisters. She may find it harder to get along with an older brother of brothers, although she may attract him more easily. An only child would be a poor match unless the man were considerably older than she or if his father were himself an oldest brother. The youngest sister of sisters may need family or hired help in her mothering. If her husband is helpful with the children, she will find mothering much easier. Her best woman friend will be an older sister of sisters or a middle sister who had a younger sister herself. She is also compatible with oldest and youngest sisters of brothers.

The Oldest Sister of Brothers

The oldest sister of brothers is independent and strong. She enjoys taking care of men and does not ask for much in return, except that the men around her be satisfied. The men in her life are her main concern. At work she often feels superior but does not show it. She can create an atmosphere that is appreciated at work. She can give advice to even the boss because she does not compete with men and actually may facilitate their relationships. She is less interested in women. She is optimistic and seems to need the companionship of men. Material possessions do not motivate her as much as possessing men, but she can administer properties and wealth well. She may be the sponsoring benefactor of gifted men. Her best marital partner would be the youngest brother of sisters, a youngest brother of brothers, or a middle brother who has at least one older sister. An only child would work if his own father was himself a youngest brother. An oldest brother of brothers might lead to a power struggle. She loves caring for children and may tend to favor sons over daughters. She may express occasional frustration with her husband's seeming passivity in the family. Friendships with women are unimportant to her, but the most compatible tends to be with the youngest sister of sisters.

The Youngest Sister of Brothers

The youngest sister of brothers is the most attractive of all the sibling positions to men. She is all that a man would conventionally wish from a woman; feminine, friendly, sympathetic, sensitive, and tactful. She is a good pal but may be a bit spoiled or extravagant. She is not ambitious for her own sake but may become so for the sake of an ambitious partner. She is not interested in work but can become motivated by the man she loves. Property and wealth do not interest her, but she is usually well taken care of by brothers or husband. The man in her life is her real wealth. She is attractive and charming to men and they instinctively seek her company. Her best marriage choice is ordinarily an oldest brother of sisters. A youngest brother of brothers or an only child would be the least favorable matches, especially if his father had been an only child or a youngest brother. She makes a loving mother but may be seen by her children as being too dependent or seductive. She is more interested in her husband than her children. She fosters the role of gentleman and protector in her sons. Daughters learn well from her how to be feminine, impress men, subordinate oneself, or get what one wants from men. Women friends are not important to her. They may envy her for her good fortune with men and her long-lasting relationships with them, which come naturally to her.

The Female Only Child

As with the male only child, the female only child tends to structure her life around older people, people in authority and superiors. Her strongest motivation is to obtain their approval and hopefully their preferential treatment. If she gets these things, she can be a good companion. Female only children tend to believe that their parents owe them help and support long into their adult years. Without a patron to champion her cause, her career may falter. Even with a patron, she may not do as well in a career as her male counterpart. Material wealth is not as motivating to her as the attention of a patron. She may be seen as spoiled or egocentric in her dealings with men. Her mother may assist her in matchmaking and may come as part of the package in her marriage. The female only child can be a good wife and is not inclined to become unfaithful. Her best partner would be the oldest brother of sisters. An oldest brother of brothers may provide the fatherly guidance she expects. A youngest or middle brother of sisters may offer her understanding of women and it will help if he is somewhat older than she. Unfavorable partners would be a youngest brother of brothers or a male only child, unless special circumstances prevailed or the spouses worked out a functional living arrangement rather than an intimate interaction. A greater-than-average age distance between the two would help, as would early identification of the husband with a father who had been an oldest sibling. A female only child prefers to be a child rather than to have children. If her mother or a mother substitute is available to help, her mothering will be facilitated. The female only child enjoys women friends, especially if they assume a motherly role toward her. She will enjoy the relationship more if they are older than she or if they are oldest sisters of sisters. She does better with individual contacts with her women friends than in groups.

Special Sibling Positions

In addition to the ten classical positions described by Dr. Toman, there are two other positions that, because of their complexity or infrequency, deserve special mention.

The Middle Child

Middle siblings may hold more than one role, since they relate differently to their younger and older siblings. Quite often one of these roles will be the strongest or will have been held for a longer period of time. This will continue to be the predominant role. In general, the siblings immediately adjacent to the middle child in age will be more important. In large families, siblings tend to form into subgroups. In such a case, a middle sibling may sometimes become a quasi-oldest or quasi-youngest.

Twins

As a rule twins live with each other from birth on and have experiences different from those of other siblings. As a result of family influences, one may function as the older—the senior in charge—and the other the junior—the impulsive and dependent one. They frequently meet the world as a pair, and they find it hard to imagine life without the other. When twins have other siblings, both of them take on the characteristic and behavior that an individual would in their sibling position. When the twins are, say, the oldest boys and have two younger sisters and a younger brother, they learn to take the roles of oldest brothers of brothers and sisters. When the twins are girls and have come after an oldest sister, both of them are likely to assume the features of younger sisters of sisters. Thus, they should be viewed as siblings in their relationship with each other, and they are likely to adopt the social behavior and interaction preferences that correspond to their overall sibling position.

The description of twins applies to triplets and quadruplets (which are rare enough to make common trends less easy to study), but their relationships to each other are more complex and variegated. They remain more detached from other siblings than do twins, and there is more environmental focus on them, which changes the family life significantly.

Resulting Relationships

How do the different sibling positions interact when they are combined in relationships? Dr. Toman's "duplication theorem" says: "Other things being equal, new social relationships tend to be more enduring and successful the more they resemble the earlier and earliest (intrafamilial) social relationships of the person involved." In his studies of thousands of relationships, Dr. Toman found that some combinations of sibling positions were complementary, that is, the people in these positions seemed to have an easier time making their relationships work, whereas other combinations were noncomplementary and, therefore, required harder work when combined in relationships.

Positions Without Rank or Sex Conflict

There are two position mixes that are totally complementary. They are:

An Oldest Brother of Sisters and Youngest Sister of Brothers
This is usually a good relationship. These two people understand each other, rarely quarrel, and supplement each other in tasks. If they marry and have children, they will be attentive and thoughtful parents. The father will set the tone in the household, but he is friendly and tolerant, while the mother is soft and submissive.

A Youngest Brother of Sisters and Oldest Sister of Brothers

This, too, is a good relationship with good mutual understanding between the two; the woman is the one who sets the tone for the relationship. The man likes the woman's advice and needs her encouragement. If these two marry and have a family, they will usually agree on issues concerning the children. She makes most of the decisions but keeps him informed. He usually consents.

Partial Sex Conflict

Four relationship patterns have a partial sex conflict. They are:

Oldest Brother of Sisters and Youngest Sister of Sisters

This is a relatively good relationship. Though the woman may have some trouble getting used to living with a man, he can usually teach her. She may oppose him or compete with him, but struggles are short-lived. He sets the tone in the family, and she obeys him—with occasional balkiness. She will need to continue contacts with her women friends and sisters.

Youngest Brother of Sisters and Oldest Sister of Sisters

This relationship is relatively good. These two are prone to get along with each other, although consorting with a male peer requires adjustment on her part. She is slightly more authoritarian than he would like, but his sense of humor will win the day. She sets the tone in the family, perhaps a bit too seriously. If they marry and have children, the children may ally with their father and feel he is one of them. The woman is interested in justice and order in her family. She must have the opportunity to keep up her feminine contacts and stay busy with some responsibilities outside the family.

Oldest Brother of Brothers and Youngest Sister of Brothers

A relatively favorable relationship. He may be too tough or self-righteous with her and inadvertently treat her as a younger brother. She usually knows how to tone him down, however, and so in time he becomes more open to her concerns. This is partly taught to him by her brothers. He enjoys pleasing her and may learn to satisfy his leadership needs more at work and with their children if they marry and have a family. He will need to maintain contacts with male friends on regular terms throughout his life.

Youngest Brother of Brothers and Oldest Sister of Brothers

Again, a relatively good relationship. The man is a follower as long as he is not patronized. He is able to accept a woman's leadership and guardianship more willingly than a man's. She may tend to mother him. He wants most of all to be understood. She treats him like one of their children, if they marry and have children. His sense of humor sometimes makes for surprises. He will continue to desire contact with male friends throughout their relationship.

Rank or Sex Conflict Relationships

There are four relationships that have either rank or sex conflicts. They are:

Oldest Brother of Sisters and Oldest Sister of Brothers

This relationship is moderately favorable. These people have learned to live with peers of the opposite sex when growing up, but both of them are oldest siblings, so they will tend to get into power struggles with each other. Each wants the other to give in, and each finds it difficult to do that. Dividing their tasks may help things.

Youngest Brother of Sisters and Youngest Sister of Brothers

This relationship is moderately good. Each person is experienced with peers of the opposite sex, but each is looking for leadership and responsibility from the other. Neither seems quite capable of providing this. Each was dependent on a sibling of the other sex while growing up. Each requires understanding but does not feel understood.

Oldest Brother of Brothers and Youngest Sister of Sisters

A moderately favorable relationship in which both people complement each other by the age rank of their sibling positions. Since the man is the oldest and the woman the youngest, the problem of neither of them having had a sibling of the opposite sex is somewhat ameliorated. He tends to take the lead in this relationship, but their situation remains tense for a rather long time, although it can be exciting in the beginning. She wants his advice and leadership role and yet finds herself resenting it from time to time. If they marry and have children, she accepts a female relative's help readily. It is important for both people to maintain contact with their same-sex friends.

Youngest Brother of Brothers and Oldest Sister of Sisters

A moderately good relationship, although neither he nor she has experienced a relationship with an opposite sex sibling while growing up. He submits to her leadership, which may become unnecessarily strict or brusque. He will occasionally compete with her until he feels listened to by her. If they marry and have children, they do not agree on how to advise them. Both partners will need to retain contact with their same-sex friends and acquaintances.

Rank and Partial Sex Conflict Relationships

There are four relationship positions with rank and partial sex conflicts. They are:

Oldest Brother of Sisters and Oldest Sister of Sisters

This is a more difficult relationship. The partners will tend to be engaged in a power struggle. The woman has not been accustomed to life with a peer of the opposite sex, and she is not very prone to learn this from her husband. He tends to be more sympathetic and tolerant, and she more rigid and strict. She will enjoy not giving up her job or career completely if they marry and have children, but it will work best if they don't work together.

Youngest Brother of Sisters and Youngest Sister of Sisters

Again, a difficult relationship because only the male has learned in his original family how to deal with a peer of the opposite sex. However, his expectations for nurturing and care rather than opposition, leadership rather than competition, may be frustrated. The woman is not sure whether to compete or submit. She tends to be critical of her husband's inadequacies. She may keep searching for an older brother to serve as an extra friend.

Oldest Brother of Brothers and Oldest Sister of Brothers

A difficult relationship because both are order-givers and responsible and both find it difficult to give in. Only the woman has been accustomed to life with peers of the opposite sex as she grew up. She could give guidance in this, but her husband is unlikely to listen. If they marry and have children, he will be more strict and she will be more lenient. They will each need juniors and dependents to care for. Their conflicts with each other will be reduced if they pursue their own interests independently.

Youngest Brother of Brothers and Youngest Sister of Brothers

A difficult relationship because only the woman knows from her experience while growing up how to handle a peer of the opposite sex. Both partners, being youngest, are searching for guidance and parental attention, but neither knows how to give it. He may be looking for a woman, as an additional friend, who is an older sister. She may need support from one of her brothers.

Rank and Sex Conflict Relationships

There are two relationship patterns with both rank and sex conflict. They are:

Oldest Brother of Brothers and Oldest Sister of Sisters

An unfavorable relationship because their own sibling experiences have not prepared either partner for life with a peer of the opposite sex. Also, there is a rank conflict for both; each will expect the other to submit, but neither is qualified for that role. Their conflict may be described as a battle of the sexes. Separate careers may help the situation. They will each need to retain their same-sex friends throughout the relationship. Temporary leaves from each other and separate rooms may help also. If they marry and have children, their relationship may seem to improve although they will be exacting parents and tend to recruit the same-sex children into alliances.

Youngest Brother of Brothers and Youngest Sister of Sisters

Again, unfavorable because of sibling experiences that put them in a relationship where both, being accustomed to being taken care of and guided as they were growing up, will tend to expect more leadership from the other than is naturally possible. Each also have had no experience living with a peer of the opposite sex. The partnership lacks leadership and direction for decision-making. If they marry, having children will not make life much easier for them. They may find some direction in their own extended families. Separate professions, interests, and pursuit of talents independently of each other may help. They will also need to maintain same-sex friendships on a fairly regular basis.

Only Children

Only children in relationships will probably do better if they marry someone who has had sibling exposure while growing up and try to learn about how to get along in peer relationships. The only child relating in a marriage will be especially helped by a partner who has had peers of the opposite sex. If both people in the relationship are only children, they will each be looking for a parental friend in one another but rarely find it. At least they can identify with one another in the longing to have parental approval. Because of this identification, they may develop a smoother relationship. If two only children marry and have a child, they may tend to concentrate more intense hopes in the child than do other parents.

Index

abuse, physical, 45
action in crisis, 137
addiction, xvi, 23, 131, 159
addiction in children, 154
Adult Children of Divorce, 178
alpha rhythm, 128
alpha wave training, 132
"An Odyssey Toward Science," 172
anger, 39
Annie Hall, 89
asthma, 132
attachment, unresolved, 60
autogenic training, 127
automatic guidance system, 20

basic self, 18
Beal, E., 178
"Biophilia," 172
biofeedback, 176
blood pressure, 132
borrowing of self, 41, 90
boundaries, 152
Bowen, Murray, biography, vii;
    Foreword, xii
brain, reptilian, 82
Buss, Leo, 173

Calhoun, John B., 165
cancer, emotional shock related
    to, 136
cerebral cortex, 27
child-focused relationships, 154
Chimpanzee Politics, 28, 174

chimpanzees at Gombe, 19
*Clinical Handbook
    of Marital Therapy,* 173
communication with children, 153
communication, elements of, 106
communism, 14
*Concepts of Science
    from Newton to Einstein,* 175
conflict resolution among
    nations, 166
conflicted relationship, 43
contact in animals, 50
court system, 165
creativity, 109, 132
crime, xvi

Darwin, Charles, xviii
democracy, 14
depressed thinking, 150
depression, 39
    after divorce, 156
    in children, 154
    in overfunctioning/
        underfunctioning, 65
    related to cutoff, 60
deWaal, Frans, 28, 30, 174, 175,
diabetes, 132
diagram, family, 9
differentiation of self, 14, 35
    scale, 186
distancing, patterns of, 53
divorce, xvi, 41, 55, 154, 156
dysfunctional spouse posture, 67

CHRONIMED Publishing Books of Related Interest

☐ **Healing the Body Betrayed: A Self-Paced, Self-Help Guide to Regaining Psychological Control of Your Chronic Illness** by Robert A. Klein, Ph.D., and Marcia Goodman Landau, Ph.D. Here's the first book to introduce the specific steps necessary to control the emotional ups and downs of a chronic illness, regardless of the specific disease. Through 50 years' clinical experience, the authors provide authoritative solutions to common problems—and show how to live the fullest life possible.
004098, ISBN 1-56561-003-2, $12.95

☐ **Diagnosing Your Doctor** by Arthur R. Pell, Ph.D. Authoritative, straightforward, and powerful, this book tells how to get the most from doctors and medical professionals—and shows you how to ask tough questions to get the right answers.
004090, ISBN 0-937721-87-5, $9.95

☐ **Minute Health Tips: Medical Advice and Facts at a Glance** by Thomas Welch, M.D. This valuable and easy-to-use guide discusses routine health problems, offers preventive medicine tips, shows you how to make doctor visits more informational, and much more.
004088, ISBN 0-937721-85-9, $8.95

☐ **Doctor, Why Do I Hurt So Much?** by Mark H. Greenberg, M.D., Lucille Frank, M.D., and Jackson Braider. This revolutionary guide will show you how to find relief from symptoms of more than 100 different types of arthritis (and dozens of other related illnesses) as well as the causes.
004091, ISBN 0-937721-88-3, $14.95

☐ **Emergency Medical Treatment: Infants—A Handbook of What to Do in an Emergency to Keep an Infant Alive Until Help Arrives** by Stephen Vogel, M.D., and David Manhoff, produced in cooperation with the National Safety Council. This easy-to-follow, step-by-step guide tells exactly what to do during the most common, life-threatening situations you might encounter for infants. Fully illustrated and indexed with thumb tabs.
004582, ISBN 0-916363-01-5, $7.95

☐ **Emergency Medical Treatment: Children— A Handbook of What to Do in an Emergency to Keep a Child Alive Until Help Arrives** by Stephen Vogel, M.D., and David Manhoff, produced in cooperation with the National Safety Council. This easy-to-follow, step-by-step guide tells exactly what to do during the most common, life-threatening situations you might encounter for children. Fully illustrated and indexed with thumb tabs.
004583, ISBN 0-916363-00-7, $7.95

☐ **Emergency Medical Treatment: Adults— A Handbook of What to Do in an Emergency to Keep an Adult Alive Until Help Arrives by** Stephen Vogel, M.D., and David Manhoff, produced in cooperation with the National Safety Council. This easy-to-follow, step-by-step guide tells exactly what to do during the most common, life-threatening situations you might encounter for adults. Fully illustrated and indexed with thumb tabs.
004584, ISBN 0-916363-05-8, $7.95

□ **The Physician Within** by Catherine Feste. Here internationally renowned health motivation specialist, Cathy Feste, focuses on motivating those with a health challenge, and anyone else, to stay on their regimen and follow healthy behavior.
004019, ISBN 0-937721-19-0, $8.95

□ **It's Your Body** by Paul Terry, Ph.D., and Allan Kind, M.D., F.A.C.P. Here are the latest facts on every facet of preventive medicine—from new ways of avoiding cancer to curbing risks during pregnancy. Complete with the newest guidelines from the American College of Physicians and the U.S. Preventive Services Task Force.
004203, ISBN 1-56561-007-5, $9.95

Buy them at your local bookstore or use this convenient coupon for ordering.

CHRONIMED Publishing
P.O. Box 47945
Minneapolis, MN 55447-9727

Please send me the books I have checked above. I am enclosing $_____. (Please add $3.00 to this order to cover postage and handling. Minnesota residents add 6.5% sales tax.) Send check or money order, no cash or C.O.D.'s. Prices are subject to change without notice.

Name _____

Address _____

City _____ State _____ Zip _____

Allow 4 to 6 weeks for delivery.
Quantity discounts available upon request.

Or order by phone: 1-800-848-2793,
1-800-444-5951 (non-metro area of Minnesota)
612-546-1146 (Minneapolis/St. Paul metro area).

Please have your credit card number ready.